Betty Kilgour

Detselig Enterprises Ltd.
Calgary, Alberta

Crocus Coulee in Bloom

© 1993 Betty Kilgour

Canadian Cataloguing in Publication Data

Kilgour, Betty.
    Crocus Coulee in bloom

    ISBN 1-55059-073-1

    1. Kilgour, Betty—Anecdotes.   2. Farm life—
Alberta—Anecdotes.   I. Title.
PS8571.I436C7 1993   971.23'3   C93-091910-6
PR9199.3.K54C37 1993

                    Detselig Enterprises Ltd.
                    210, 1220 Kensington Rd. NW
                    Calgary, Alberta T2N 3P5

Cover and inside illustrations by Ben Crane

Printed in Canada   ISBN 1-55059-073-1   SAN 115-0324

for Bill
with love

Author's Acknowledgements

When a book is published many experts besides the author are instrumental in its completion and so it is with *Crocus Coulee in Bloom*.

Again a hearty thank you to Detselig – I'm truly blessed with a wonderful publisher and staff:

Ted Giles, for believing in me and my writing skills yet again. Sherry Wilson McEwen, my editor, for her ability to polish, adjust and create in such a pleasant manner. May Misfeldt, Linda Berry, Barry Rust and Suzette Mayr for their friendship and help.

A big thank you to Ben Crane, my illustrator, who once again came up with a wonderful cover and some truly amazing illustrations! Thank you to Ted Bower – one of my very favorite newspaper editors while I wrote for the Red Deer Advocate – for kindly writing the foreword.

Also, many thanks to the various newspapers and magazines in which some of the stories were published through the years, especially the *Red Deer Advocate*, the *Alberta Farm and Ranch* and the *Canadian Hereford Digest*.

And most of all, thanks to all my family – how could I ever complete my various projects without your help and sustaining love? Thanks to Pat for her computer skills and the rest for their support.

Publisher's Acknowledgement

Financial support for Detselig Enterprises Ltd. 1993 publishing program is provided by the Department of Communications, Canada Council and The Alberta Foundation for the Arts, a beneficiary of the Lottery Fund of the Government of Alberta.

Contents

Spring in Bloom

Summertime in the Country

Fall on the Farm

Winter Sports

Foreword

The wonderful thing about Betty Kilgour – her latest book is in your hands – is that she has the courage to be her stubborn, hilarious self, in print. She has convictions. She is funny and wholesome as homemade bread. She doesn't whine. She can be naive and touching and wise. She can be outrageous. Her most noble strength is tolerance. She is a farm woman who writes with kindly humor, taking kitchen-table anecdotes and shaping them into short stories about rural Alberta life, spanning the decades from the 1940s to the nineties.

I first heard of Betty when my mother, who was a great reader and relished a good story, came across some Kilgour stories in a farm paper. She knew farm life and Betty Kilgour's stories had a resonance for her. At the time, I was editor of a small newspaper with many rural readers. One day, in one of life's fortuitous coincidences, a batch of Betty Kilgour stories arrived on my desk. Would I be interested in a weekly Kilgour column, leavened with first-hand vignettes about farm life?

To my surprise and delight, I learned the writer was virtually a neighbor: Betty Kilgour and her husband farmed at a place called Crocus Coulee, near Three Hills in central Alberta, which was in my newspaper's circulation area. I sampled her columns and this farmboy-turned-journalist was smitten. Betty Kilgour was her own woman; these were nostalgia stories with an authentic ring. It was my joy that rural readers (and some folk with rural roots) enjoyed her tales, recounted in an unvarnished, madcap style. (At times, to be sure, she was the despair of language purists but then, what do language purists know about such kitchen-table topics as calving or combines or chokecherries or caraganas?) Ultimately, the cream of her early columns reappeared in book form, *The Best Of Crocus Coulee*.

Now the wheel has come around again. There were more columns after the first book and here's a selection of the best, with Betty Kilgour's humor illuminating life's little moments on the farm. These days, her stories have a grandmother's perspective and are burnished by experiences when she and her husband served overseas as CUSO volunteers in Africa and the

South Pacific – adventures that yielded three more Kilgour books, expanded horizons and new friendships.

Betty Kilgour is one of a kind, an amazing Albertan and we're all the better for her inimitable energy. Enjoy!

– *Ted Bower*

❀❀❀❀❀❀❀❀❀
Of Olden Days
❀❀❀❀❀❀❀❀❀

❀ ❀ ❀ ❀ ❀ ❀ ❀ ❀

Old-time Schools

❀ ❀ ❀ ❀ ❀ ❀ ❀ ❀

Whenever I leave our homestead, Crocus Coulee, to go into town and I pass the local school, I do so with mixed feelings. "Oh I wish I had the opportunity to go to such a school!" but "These kids of today didn't have the fun we had!"

Sure, schools now have amazing pluses. Carpeting in every room, bright lights which are never turned off, computers, libraries with hundreds of books. Some of the halls are wider than some old classrooms I attended!

I don't for one moment believe the kids of today are brighter or are learning more than we did – but boy, the surroundings are certainly more luxurious.

Instead of carpeted floors we had good sturdy wood ones which were oiled every month to keep the dust down and to frustrate all the mothers on wash day.

These floors passed out slivers religiously, without fear or favor. So many, in fact, that we kids would save them and the one with the longest was top dog. There was no prize as such, just a rather dubious honor. I won it but once, playing *PUM PUM PULLAWAY*. I went into a seven-foot sli-i-i-de and the sliver was a whopper. The honor achieved was only slightly dampened by the visit to the doctor to get that piece of floor dug out of me!

Possibly the most humble hall of learning I attended was a one-room country school where I spent my primary-grade years. This little school, so like hundreds of others dotted across the western prairies, was a washed out, weather-beaten building squatting on a hill. It housed kids from grade 1 to grade 8. To my knowledge two lawyers, a doctor, a nurse and three teachers emerged from that homely, humble building.

It had five windows to the east and was situated seven yards from the gate. This I know for sure. I was a rather shy child when it came to reading out loud in front of the class – not a soul could hear me. In fact the only way to see if I was actually reading was to watch my lips and see if they were moving. The teacher stood this quirk as long as he could but one day he blew and sent me out to that gate and made me read loud enough for him to hear inside the school. I didn't overcome this shyness that year but I did get lots of fresh air and also wore a deep path between the school and the gate.

Our school drinking supply was kept in an old rusty bucket. We thought nothing of everyone drinking from the same chipped enamel dipper. I guess our bugs were of all the same strain. Mononucleosis was unheard of – the odd case of ring-worm maybe!

In the morning we all took on a good stout drink of water when it was fresh and cool because we knew by three p.m. it looked like used dishwater and tasted of sulphur. In fact it would take near dehydration to force any of us to even take a sip.

Our school heating system was not "state of the art" – instead it was one big black potbellied heater which ate moun-tains of wood during the winter. It was the job of one grade 8 boy and three grade 4 boys to appease this monster's appetite! On top of this stove sat an old tin can which the teacher kept full of water and creolin. This was supposed to kill all the germs and keep the winter flu at bay. We got so used to the smell that when spring finally arrived we found fresh air hard to breathe.

Lighting was not of great importance. The windows pro-vided most of the light and if a dust storm blew in three kerosene lamps were lit. We loved a dust storm because even with the lamps we couldn't see to do any serious studying. One dust storm lasted almost an hour and so we had a semi-concert. Three boys sang Wilf Carter songs, we had a recitation and three fights the teacher didn't even see.

Lunches varied but little. No fancy Smurf lunch boxes or thermoses. We had old lard tins or Roger's Golden Syrup cans holding a sandwich sometimes made with lard and homemade jam, sometimes a boiled egg and a piece of Johnny Cake. At Christmas time we might have an orange, the ultimate treat.

The plumbing was nil. There were two outside biffys instead, one for the girls and one for the boys. Our tissue was old catalogues and the walls were covered with sayings which I didn't understand for years! The most exciting moment of the year was once when a muskrat inadvertently got down the hole of the girls' toilet. The noise the girl who spotted the creature made was truly amazing.

We didn't have a library as such but we did have three books and a dictionary. One book was *Wuthering Heights* and the other two were Zane Greys. There was a wonderful world map hanging on the wall. This was issued by the Neilsen

Chocolate company and decorating each corner was a picture of their different chocolate bars. To my child's mind they were real – just setting there, ready to be grasped. My faith in humanity was shot the day I finally got up enough courage to walk up and touch one corner. Woe of woes, they were fake. It was all a mirage – just cheap old drawings! My I was disappointed! This sadness lasted until I found a secret wild strawberry patch in the corner of the school yard. To this precious spot I retired each and every recess. Who wanted chocolate bars when you could eat strawberries anyway?

Cooking Then and Now

❀ ❀ ❀ ❀ ❀ ❀ ❀ ❀ ❀ ❀ ❀

As a young bride, when I first moved to Crocus Coulee, I was no cook. It mattered little what I cooked, it was a surprise and not always a pleasant one. I had taken Home Ec. That was little help when all I remembered cooking there was Spanish Cream. But first blown love is wonderful and I do believe there's one special guardian angel who looks after new husbands. So with a great deal of perseverance on both our parts, I learned the art of cooking. There was just the two of us and some meals were a little weird but by the time a year was up I could toss up a basic meal.

I knew the quantities to cook and the amount of groceries to buy and was quite enjoying my kitchen.

By then we decided to get hired help. We had bought cattle and just couldn't keep up with all the chores and land work. Of course I had to learn how to cook larger quantities as our help were young men with huge appetites who could eat anything set in front of them. There would be no more cornflake suppers or hamburgers bought in town. And if you are a farmer's wife you learn fast. Otherwise you get marked down as a rotten cook in the Farmer's Sorority and that is a fate worse than death! Soon I got the feel of it. I knew what I needed and became a bit more daring with my recipes.

While I was practising all this our family was growing so I had to keep on increasing the amounts. Half the recipes I had were so small I found myself jotting down double and even triple amounts on the recipe card. I'd think nothing of using six cups of flour instead of two and I found myself buying giant cookie sheets and pots you could feed fifty from. It was as if I was on a food treadmill – the more I cooked, the more was eaten.

As our kids grew our grocery bills kept up. A case of this, a carton of that. Flour was bought in 100-pound sacks and sugar in 50-pound. I grew enough vegetables to feed an army and canned and pickled like crazy.

Our grocery order was so huge that when Bill packed it out the back door of the store, other customers would stand with mouths agape at our order, wondering if we were feeding the Salvation Army. I got tired of trying to explain that five kids, three hired men, an assortment of friends and the cat and dog eat a lot.

It was not unusual to mix a batch of cookies in the sink because it was so large. I remember mixing a wedding cake for one of our daughters in a washtub.

Then the kids grew up and left for jobs in the city and I had to cut back. I kept my paring knife under wraps so I didn't peel twenty potatoes instead of six. I had to buy three-pound roasts instead of six and go back to single batches. I hated it. It cramped my style. I'd make great pots of soup and freeze it and bake seven cakes at a blow but even the deep freeze complained. This short period of my life was not happy.

But now, with the family all married and some able to come each lunch and a score of new kids and grand kids, I'm back in my element. I dragged out all the big pots and pans and take my grocery list in with a flourish. I heard someone say last week when I was purchasing, "My what does she do with all those groceries? Does she ever forget anything?"

Another thing I hear often is, "Why there is just the two of you now. Why do you buy like that?" as the woman waves a hand at my heap.

"Lady," I'd like to say, "there is never a day when we do not have extra at our table. They are all welcome and I couldn't be happier!"

Now I'd better go make a triple batch of cabbage rolls just in case!

Grandmother's Recipes

Remember the old recipes our grandmothers used to make? Usually written down in an old 5 cent scribbler or on the back of last year's calendar pages,they were collected from friends and relatives. The odd one was improvised on the spot if ingredients were short.

Special titles were created for these recipes, with comments added after the initial test.

"Jack's Favorite Pickle" (*Keep in cellar*)

"Judy's Candy" (*Easy to make*)

Certain pages came loose after much handling and the odd recipe, usually a favorite, was often well spotted with old dough. The ingredients were easily measured but the style would drive a Home Economist nuts! A dash of salt, butter the size of an egg, flour enough to stiffen, bake 'til done! And that's what Grandma did!

Many recipes were concocted during the great Depression in the 1930s. Of course young children back then didn't realize the times were tough and food often scarce – they just acquired a taste for whatever was cooked up.

I remember one recipe my mother used to make – Turnip Relish. I loved the stuff and would slather it on bread, mix it with my macaroni, even eat it by the spoonful right out of the jar. I didn't know what it was made of but to me it was fit for a Queen.

When I was first married, I asked Mother for the recipe. She hesitated.

"Don't you remember making it?" I asked her.

"Yes I do, but I really didn't have a recipe!"

What she gave me were the basic ingredients: Swede turnips, sugar, spices and vinegar. We figured out appropriate amounts and I set about making this ambrosia from my childhood dreams. I could hardly wait for it to cool! As I tried it on a slice of bread I pictured my self back in Sundre sitting on the back step; as I ate I realized one should never try to relive a dream. I was so disappointed – it didn't taste anything like that wonderful stuff from long ago. I guess I had built it up to such an extent nothing short of heavenly manna would have pleased me.

The wonderful thing about Grandma's recipes is the fact that they make such dandy big batches and are simplicity itself.

Grandma had so many other chores to do she didn't waste time with a lot of sifting and measuring if she could make it just as well without.

Exotic spices or fancy ingredients were seldom used; oh maybe at Christmas time or for a wedding reception, but in her day any but the very basic ingredients were just too expensive.

There were no mixes back then and even if there had been, I don't think she would have used them. Even when Certo came on the market, she scoffed at it. I remember her saying, on see me using it by the bottle in my jam-making sessions, "You don't get the flavor using that – it needs the extra boil!"

Still in all, I've got two ancient scribblers full of old-time recipes which I use often. If I have the need of a huge cake that takes the bare necessities, I always fall back on those books.

I also have got in the habit of rarely measuring, never sifting and never timing the baking of anything. I'm like Grandma. I just bake 'til done!'

The Caragana Hedge

Most people today, if confronted with a caragana hedge, immediately think "weed" or "damned nuisance" and proceed to have it unceremoniously pulled out by the roots. I can understand these feelings. I have had such a hedge pulled out myself.

The feeling today is, these shrubs use up much needed moisture, they disperse seedlings for many yards into places they are not wanted, and it's impossible to keep them under control. If caragana surround your yard all the junk blows in and gets stuck in the hedge, making it impossible to rake out in the spring. When you reach in to get this stuff manually you get scratched to death. No – pull them out and plant some of the gentler varieties of shrubs now available.

Still, the caragana had its day. I believe every school I attended had a caragana hedge and every church too. The houses in small towns across the prairies were divided by such a hedge and many farmsteads used them for a windbreak.

Probably the reason they were so popular was because they were cheap, available and would grow anywhere. Besides that, you couldn't kill them. They were the ultimate survivor, a point much admired by the early gardeners. Anything which with-stood our cold winter year after year demanded respect.

In fact, if you drive about you'll generally see at each old homestead site, although the buildings are gone, a healthy caragana bush or two.

These bushes bring back memories to many, I'm sure. I know as little kids my good chum June and I picked buckets of seed pods from her folks' caragana hedge. You see we were hoping to make heaps of money out of the exquisite jewellery we were about to fashion out of the seed pods. The picking was the most difficult.

"I've got my bottom covered!" we'd shout back and forth. Our clothes were ripped and our arms scratched and bleeding. The pods were tenacious things and wished only to cling to the branches. However, we had boasted to all our friends about going into the jewellery business which we were sure was going to be profitable and we weren't going to give up this early.

Once we had them picked we'd sit on June's back step stringing them into what we fully expected to be works of art. For this we used number 20 black-and-red thread and our Moms' needles. We had a few sequins we found in a sewing machine drawer so we'd slip one in here and there between the pods for added beauty.

Actually there was scant beauty in the creations we had strung but to our juvenile eyes they looked quite wonderful and worth at least two dollars a string.

We worked for days, hurrying even with the dishes so we could string some more before the sun set. Our mothers wouldn't let us in the house with them so we had limited time.

As we worked, we planned as only seven-years-olds can. We'd get the address of the King and Queen and send them one necklace for each of their daughters. I'm not sure how much Princess Margaret would have appreciated our efforts, never mind Elizabeth but we had, if not great talent, at least immense entrepreneurial spirit!

Sadly, the bottom fell out of our market, as well as our hopes, the first time we tried to sell some. We went down to the local general store where, when we held them up, the seeds all fell out of the pods. The manager had the audacity to laugh at us, pat our heads and give us each a jawbreaker.

Next we decided we'd at least make a meager living witching water wells for the farmers. We had seen a big Swede who lived in the next town witch a well. It was almost magical – his immense arms couldn't hold that stick even though he was trying so hard to contain it he broke out in a sweat and groaned in pain! It had a real effect on us, especially when the well turned out to be a gusher!

Naturally it was to the caragana we turned for the forked stick we needed. We picked several and peeled them lovingly. Then we hit for the slough at the edge of town. We figured we could practise near water and then when we excelled at it we could move inland, to wherever our talents were needed.

We walked back and forth trying to stir up a tingle. After what seemed like hours of plodding about until our arms felt like they were about to fall off, my stick magically seemed to point downwards. A vast underground stream, we said. But we were hungry and tired and by the time we got home we had lost heart.

Every spring we'd sit on the grass and watch the blackbirds and wild canaries build their nests in the hedge. Later, we'd peek carefully into the nest to see if the eggs had hatched.

The caragana hedge was also useful as a stopper if your bike didn't have brakes. And you could hide in it or hide a belonging in it so not a soul would ever find it or you.

Oh yes, your old caragana hedge could tell many a tale. No prairie kids of the thirties or forties was raised without one of these old friends.

The Vacant Lot

As I get older I realize I had access to some wonderful freebies as a kid.

One of these was a real old-fashioned vacant lot only four houses from home. To an adult it must have been an eyesore – weeds knee high, old boxes and broken glass scattered throughout. To us kids it was a regular amusement park.

A vacant lot was pure unadulterated fun. Through the long, lazy summer months it held the whole gang to its bosom. We didn't see the junk and weeds – we saw a fairyland.

I well remember mothers using it as a babysitter. Their pre-schoolers would be sent out to play with orders to stay within the confines of the old lot, or else. Our moms found it a trusted friend. No danger from traffic, close to home and harmless.

We'd play with our dolls and the boys with their trucks climbing imaginary mountains over the clumps of dirt. We couldn't care less if it had thistles and the dandelions were used as our wedding bouquets.

As we grew older, we used this lot for games, testing our imagination to the hilt. The lot became the open plains with cowboys and Indians fighting it out.

We took turns, the cowboys winning one battle and the Indians the next. We used to swipe our mothers' make-up to use as war paint. This we plastered on so thick it took three days scrubbing and one layer of skin to get it off.

We learned to skip there and play marbles. Both boys and girls played "house," to use the term loosely and oh, our homes were delightful – old blankets, hooked on to a tree branch and held down with rocks. Our kitchen supplies were collected from the bits of junk unearthed there – rusty tins, pop bottles and all sorts of other finds. The biggest find ever was the shell of an old Winnipeg couch – that we used for years.

I mustn't forget the games of doctor and nurse. We took turns playing doctor and patient although no one wanted to be a patient until we quit using an old rusty needle for injections. Our mothers worried about what we'd learn when we stripped for examination. I can tell you now, we all passed our biology final with nothing under 89 percent. And I might note three boys became doctors. I can't tell you how many nurses we turned out!

As we grew, the lot seemed smaller, although there was still plenty of room for our games of scrub. This lot was actually a training ground for softball. Many of our gang graduated into the lofty high-school teams, the dream of each of us. We got all the choice positions because we had practised so much on the vacant lot.

One thing I must mention is the romance department. Most every couple caught up in the throes of puppy love used the old vacant lot as their trysting spot. That place absolutely sizzled for years.

My empty lot is long gone, now. A huge new brick home rests there on the sod but the trees remain and my memory of it is clear. I'll always remember all the things I learned out on the old vacant lot.

The Old Ball Teams

Every time I see kids playing ball, I envy them. Playing ball was the passion of my life. I know if the need arose I could still catch those flies and hit at least a double. There's no team needing my capabilities at the moment but I'm waiting for the call.

When I was a little kid, ball was my life. I lived and breathed ball – nothing else mattered – not even boys. I'd play at recess, noon hour, after school and in the evenings. My weekends were one big ball game and if it rained I felt like my dog just died.

Scrub was the perennial favorite of most kids. Of course it seemed that I never got to bat. I'd start out in right field and by the time I finally got to the bag, the bell would ring or the stars would be out. I think I batted maybe ten times in two years of scrub, but I sure improved my fielding.

Later I was old enough to play on a regular team. I tried to get on the boys' team but no luck – all they allowed me to do was carry water and pick up bats. One year I was in my glory as I was on not one but three teams: 13 and under, 15 and under and the high-school girls team. Was it because of my great playing ability or because I wore the Captains down? Every time they'd turn around, there I would be. After tripping over me so many times, they'd finally weaken and stick me out in the field and try to forget about me. But with so much practise I could really field. If the ball was hit anywhere, even the next town, I'd catch it. Boy I was good!

My throwing arm wasn't that great and the hardest thing for me was learning the fine art of sliding into base. I practised and practised but couldn't master it, even though I wore out more jeans than my brother did. All I accomplished was knocking the player off base. I heard, "You clumsy oaf what are you doing?" so many times it echoed in my sleep. Each day I'd go home so battered up I looked like the victim of a cat fight. So much so my mother begged me to take up some other hobby. Maybe needlework? No dice. That would be equivalent to asking Number 99 to quit hockey.

When there wasn't a ball game or a practice, I'd go around pestering everyone from the local drayman to pregnant women to hit me out some balls to catch. I had one neighbor who was extra kind, having played ball himself as a young man. He took pity and batted for me. I'd keep him in the vacant lot all night or until he, in desperation, sent the ball flying a block away so he could beat a hasty retreat.

We didn't own uniforms back then. Instead we each had a big white sweatshirt and sewed bright red crests on them. This looked smart until the first wash, when the crests ran – I believe that was the start of tie-dying as we know it today.

It didn't bother us, though. We felt quite stylish in our mottled red shirts and baggy pants rolled up to the knee. We played all the teams in neighboring towns, sometimes winning and sometimes losing.

One ailment I had each summer was sprained fingers. All through the ball season one or two of my fingers would be swollen up like a beef sausage. I was a lefty and couldn't afford to buy the right-hand glove, only with such swollen appendages it was just like wearing one.

Oh well, some day I may play another game or two. Last year at our family reunion the grandchildren got a game going and one of my grandsons picked me for his team. My I love that boy! And by golly, I even slugged the ball a couple of times. Running was a bit difficult – I felt like someone was holding me back by my underwear but I got around the bases and felt like a new woman. I didn't tell a soul I was practically bedridden for a good week.

Still, the urge is there. Remember Grandma Moses? Yes, this southpaw is gonna rise again!!

❀ ❀ ❀ ❀ ❀ ❀ ❀ ❀

Rummage Sales

❀ ❀ ❀ ❀ ❀ ❀ ❀ ❀

Most of us love garage sales. Some spend every week-end travelling from one to another buying up what they think are wonderful purchases.

But long before garage sales became so popular we had a thing called a rummage sale. These sales were great money-makers for many a worthwhile cause. Besides they were fun: fun to prepare, fun to work at and fun to partake in.

Each an every year the local IODE sponsored a popular one. Bits and pieces of this and that were laid out on long tables in the Community Centre with a tea as a sideline. The ladies found that they could do well with a tea because by the time the customers looked, felt, held back, then purchased from six or eight turkey supper-length tables, they were gasping for a cup of tea.

For months before the event the whole district was canvassed for whatever you didn't need. Old clothes, dishes, wool, tools everything from hammers to hair dryers – nothing was turned down and most everything was sold.

It was absolutely a heady feeling to gather up all the junk which had accumulated. Why here was the chance to clear the house and still feel good about it – it was going to such a worthy cause was the magic guilt reliever.

A rummage sale is the best way to clean house. You could, for a good reason (laziness) throw in those jeans you meant to lengthen, the summer coat so old you wore it like a second skin but couldn't wear it out, that blouse Aunt Mathilda made you four Christmases ago which you hated and even that work shirt you spilt the bleach on. In any home that houses humans, things seem to collect. Our tradition seems to be never throw anything away – you just might need it later. This bodes the truth. Throw one thing out and see how quickly you wish you hadn't.

Our forefathers knew this – they recycled before the word was invented. It's part of our bloodline.

Still, a house can only handle so much. With children, even with hand-me-downs, there are things for which you can't find room. What fits one kid will inevitably be too short, too wide, too narrow for the next kid, simply because God makes all people different. Also there is only so much you can do with thread, needles and bias tape to cover hem marks.

Another problem is style – any teenager will tell you style changes every three months. So you see, a good rummage sale was the ticket.

The sale itself was always a huge success, the reason being that women have a built in trigger which goes off automatically the second they step in front of a bargain table. The very sight of such a table brings out the old instinct of self-preservation their ancestors needed to exist. The pioneer women could take an old coat, turn it inside out, remake it and presto! Young Johnny had a warm jacket bearing craftsmanship rarely seen today. She could also take Dad's old worn-out socks and produce mittens in less than half an hour. She'd make over dresses or aprons and what was left over, she made into rag rugs. I expect if there was anything left after the rug, she'd line the cat's birthing box.

So you see the old call is still within us. Besides getting rid of stuff we don't need, the sale's the spot to buy stuff we can use. An exchange of goods. The bit of yarn, the socks for the orphanage, that dish drainer you melted by accident and need to replace.

"Why there's that perfect sweater for Junior, a cub uniform for Patrick and by ginger, the perfect ear rings for Aunt Minerva's purple dress!"

Needless to say, when the loot is dragged home some items don't work. The sweater is too small, Patrick's joining 4H, and Aunt Minerva hasn't got her purple dress any more — she gave it to the rummage sale of course!

Old Club Days

❀ ❀ ❀ ❀ ❀ ❀ ❀

There are many clubs for kids these days – possibly too many. Back when I was a kid (yes there was a time) there were few clubs.

Girls could attend Explorers, then graduate to CGIT (Canadian Girls in Training). Oh it sounded grand. I still am not sure what we were in training for but I loved it so much.

This club was a God send for me as well as many others. We were poor and lived in poor times. CGIT gave us all an out, a vision possibly. It gave us one night a week to dream of lofty glories still ahead of us. And it gave us summer camp.

Part of the program was public speaking. Being so very shy I found this part devastating. When I was young, I'd cover my embarrassment in several ways – by chewing gum like I was murdering it, sucking my hair or biting my nails. In my teens I'd giggle or forget my lines.

However, we were diligently led through all sorts of plays, pageants and drills in the hope we would improve.

Only one girl in our group really liked public speaking. She excelled at it and the rest of us were jealous. We found hating her quite natural. Horrid creatures that we were, we'd sit near the front and mimic her. This was easy as she also took singing lessons as well as elocution and had been taught to open her mouth in an assortment of ways so the vowels would pop out just so. This gave us rotters ample opportunity for real mimicry.

One night during a program at the United Church we went too far and the poor girl stomped off the stage in a huff. We lost our first year chevrons and four months!

One Christmas pageant I'll never forget. We were given our parts in ample time but were too lazy to memorize them. When the big night arrived and the parents filed in to view their darlings on stage, we were paralyzed. We forgot what few lines we had learned, thoroughly disgraced ourselves and just about finished off our poor leader. The saving grace came when one bright little French girl pulled the best fainting act you ever saw. As she was carried limply from the stage we all slunk out the back door. Our poor parents were mortified and we felt so very ashamed. Believe me, we knew our lines next pageant time!

We often held drills of which we were extremely proud and really practised for. We never missed a cue and kept time beautifully.

These drills were usually performed at the annual church supper, where we were all in our glory. The odd time some of us were taken to task for chewing gum in time with our marching feet. (The height of ill manners we were told!)

As time progressed my leader – who had assured me the day would come when I would master my shyness and actually like public speaking – proved to be right. I began to feel much more at ease. We took a lot of public speaking in school and the most fun was finding subjects. The field was wide open and having quite a vivid imagination, I chose some real wonders.

While others spoke on "World affairs," "The value of home economics" and "Why I want to be a nurse," I would branch off on subjects like "Why can't we go naked?" which upset my teacher for some reason. The one which nearly finished my very Scottish father was, "Why I want to be a Hutterite."

✿ ✿ ✿ ✿ ✿ ✿ ✿

My Old Stove

✿ ✿ ✿ ✿ ✿ ✿ ✿

One thing I acquired when I married Bill and moved to Crocus Coulee was an old coal-and-wood range.

Now this wasn't something new for me, I had grown up with one of these stoves and could run it passably well. But each range is different and often temperamental and you have to get to know each one's idiosyncrasies in order to run it.

The second I entered the house as the new mistress, I was in trouble. That stove had a black and brooding soul and was bound and bent it was not going to allow some brash young thing replace its former madam (who had moved to town).

So it proceeded to make my life utter hell. It's a good thing this all happened long before the Amityville horror stories or I'd have been turned into a screaming idiot.

First of all, I tried the kid glove treatment. I polished its bosom until it glowed. I cleaned out the firebox and wiped out the oven. It should have been purring in delight but no way, for the whole of the first year it tormented me.

I'd crush paper just so and lay kindling as fine as a toothpick gently over that. Double-check the damper and then and only then light it ever so cautiously. Sometimes it would burst forth with such a flame I wouldn't have time to get the next size of wood stuffed into its mouth before the first was just a bit of ash. Other times it would sit and sulk while I used up two boxes of matches trying to coax forth a little flame. When I cautiously peeked in to see if there was any flame it would maliciously emit a great belch of smoke and ash in my face.

I'd lay different paper, tissue paper, toilet paper, even Bill's road map, trying to tempt it into action. Finally in desperation in would go an old soup can full of gas – for one whole year I was known as the woman without eyelashes.

The odd time, in utter despair, I'd tattle on it to Bill. But he'd just smile, pat me on the head and say, "Come on, honey, I'll show you how to start a fire!" Well I knew very well how to start a fire – I just didn't know how to handle something that was out to ruin my marriage!

Then Bill would do exactly the same things I always did – toss in some paper, toss a stick or two on top and the miserable wretch would blaze up like a red hot mistress batting her flames at Bill.

I never give up – I'm a very determined person, so I worked at improving relations with that stove until it finally called a truce. It would do its best if I didn't cuss or kick it.

Actually, we became quite good buddies in time and between us we turned out hundreds of cakes, breads and pies for a family of seven, three or four men, plus untold visitors over the years. The old stove seemed to savor the tidbits of garbage I fed it – I kept the reservoir full and ash pan empty.

The stove dried thousands of soggy mitts in its warming oven and toasted many cold toes on its oven door. Eventually the old stove started to show its age and could be grumpy at times. The odd time it would belch a bit and once or twice its grates fell down in its ash pan but it was a companion to all the family.

And then one day, fickle me saw a younger, electric model and fell in love. I kept this affair a secret until the poor old stove's door fell off one day, whereupon I grabbed it like a shot and tossed it out on the lawn discus-thrower style, all the while yelling for the new one. I practically had to hide my head in the broom closet as my old buddy was hauled away but oh how I looked forward to my new stove.

It didn't take long to realize the new one had no personality at all – just youthful good looks. I missed the old one, its warmth and companionship and the sound of the kettle singing away on its breast.

Oh well, I guess that's progress.

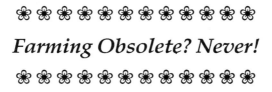

Farming Obsolete? Never!

With many farms going under these days, the media are overworking the phrase, "Farming is Obsolete." I disagree with this grand sweeping statement. Possibly it is as we know it today but heaven help the world if farming is ever obsolete.

I just don't believe it. Remember the terrible thirties and the Depression? Farmers were about the only ones holding their own. I know some settlers had to pack up and leave their land but many others hung in there. Some had city people working for them just for their room and board. One story I heard was that one of the largest hotels in Calgary was using cow pies for fuel to help keep costs down.

No, farming will never be obsolete. We *will* have to change our lifestyle. The larger farmers will have to be content to farm with older, smaller equipment or they will debt themselves to death – those payments are hard bargainers!

No matter how tough times get, if we have a couple of milk cows, fifty chickens, a pig or two and a big garden including a rhubarb patch and the saskatoons in the coulee, we won't starve. No more mansions and equipment the likes most countries have never heard of. No more holidays in Florida.

I can't help but think these are really not that important in the greater scheme of things. They really don't bring great happiness to the home as far as I can see.

Just think – we could accept the wonderful challenge of being self-sustaining! We could take wheat to the mill and need never run out of flour. What was left we could exchange for breakfast cereal. We could dig out our Grandmother's old cook books once more. These gems contain healthy, appetizing recipes with very basic ingredients.

If things get really tough, we could knit our sweaters and I have a pattern for mitts made out of the tops of old worn out socks. Our jackets would be much more basic. But then, designer labels never kept anyone warm.

If the flour mills would bring back cotton flour sacks, we'd have material for all sorts of things – dishtowels, tablecloths, even pillowcases. And wouldn't that help clean up the environment? No more plastic bags to dispose of!

Now that I'm on such a roll, how about making our own bread? When was the last time you had a slice of bread, hot from the oven, slathered with butter and jam? The butter and jam would need be homemade as well, of course. Heavens, the sky's the limit!

If all this should come about family life would change drastically for the better, I believe. Just think, we'd never hear, "I'm bored" again!

Each child would have his own chores and be responsible for his own actions – something children haven't been asked to do for too long. They would be an integral part of the family and its welfare. They could once more use their imagination – something that's also been lost in our modern world. They could make their own fun – stilts, tree houses, play houses in old chicken coops. They could enjoy reading once more, another lost art.

They would also have an interest in living things – cows, calves, pet barn cats and a dog or two. Will all this help to decrease the suicides among young people? I would hope and pray so. My goodness, I've made it all sound so wonderful, I'm looking forward to it when the time arrives!

I must say, I'm not looking forward to the cow chips for the stove idea – I might draw the line at that. Otherwise, I think it would be the salvation of many homes, physically and mentally.

There would be no more keeping up with someone else – we'd all be in the same boat and hopefully seeing that true happiness has little to do with how many cars we have or how many square feet our house contains.

No, farming is here to stay but in a much different form than what we feel is productive today.

❀❀❀❀❀❀❀❀❀❀❀❀❀

Newfangled Things

❀❀❀❀❀❀❀❀❀❀❀❀❀

Burning Husbands' Belongings

One thing I've learned over the years here at Crocus Coulee – never burn anything that belongs to your husband and I mean NEVER!

You can burn the toast, scorch the stew, burn anything else you want, as long as it's not your husband's.

For some reason, as time rolls on and the goods become more dilapidated, they also become more precious. Now I'm not talking about special heirlooms or keepsakes – no, I'm talking about worn-out junk!

My first lesson and downfall on the marital ladder was caused by an old, dirty, battered tweed cap.

It was terrible. Frayed and floppy, it looked like a dead crow on my husband's head. At least, I thought so at the time. Now I hardly notice if his head is there but back then I wanted him to be stylish.

He had this cap when I first met him and if he hadn't been such a handsome hunk and had so many other great qualities, that cap alone would have caused me to go on to other heads.

He wore it every blessed day and even on dates, to my great chagrin. People used to wonder why I was always cuddling down by the dash in the old Ford Model A. Well, the cause wasn't all romance – it was embarrassment due to that cap.

After we were married I vowed it would go out the door as I was carried in. In reality, it took slightly longer than that. He kept the thing on top of the fridge and every day I felt it snickering down at me as I went about my work.

One day Bill was off to a funeral – about the only place he didn't wear his beloved cap, so I took some matches in one hand and that old cap in the other and headed for the garbage barrel. I lit the match with great glee and watched the old thing burn.

I always wondered how people of bygone times could watch human beings burned at the stake and get some sort of thrill out of it but believe me, if that old cap had possessed a soul, I would have still enjoyed watching it go up in flame, thread by thread.

I poked about in the barrel, making sure the evidence of my dastardly deed was banished, then walked to the house with a spring in my step.

I guess I was too young or stupid to realize the very first thing Bill would look for on arriving home would be that old cap.

Sure enough, on changing his clothes, I heard a yell.

"Honey, where's my cap?"

"Which cap?" I answered, trying to sound nonchalant.

"You know which one, my work cap!"

"Did you look in the bunk house?"

This was straight-out stalling for the simple reason Bill had never in his entire life left any clothes, never mind his cap, in the bunkhouse.

I took a deep breath and said softly, "Really, honey, why not just scoot into Macleod's and get a new one?" I didn't add, "In case the old one has magically disappeared!"

"I like my old one!"

I took a deep breath. "Look, I empty the mousetraps for you, so please just go and get a nice new one for me!"

"Where's my cap?" This was said through gritted teeth. Wow, things were getting a little sticky.

I took another one of my now popular deep breaths. Throwing caution to the wind, I blurted out my guilt.

"I burnt that horrid old thing, so there!"

The look that came over my beloved's face was a mixture of surprise, hurt and indignation, with a tear tossed in for good measure.

You would have thought I had burnt his prize bull or the family dog. "Bets, how on earth could you have burnt my good cap – it belongs to me."

By this time I was getting snarky.

"Yes, and I do too, but not for long!!" I snorted and stormed off to the bedroom.

"Never touch my cap again!" he shouted and drove off to town. He came home with another, exactly the same as the first.

I held little hope of it wearing out for a good ten years, about as long as it was going to take to get back in his good graces.

I am still a maniac with the garbage barrel but now if I do, in desperation only, decide to burn something of his, I hide it first for about a month. If he hasn't missed it, I can still burn it. If not, I return it to its rightful owner.

New Corrals

❀ ❀ ❀ ❀ ❀ ❀

Corrals and stock chutes are more important to the cattleman than money to the Rockefellers. These items of wood and wire can mean the difference between staying sane and going stark mad.

They have to be kept up. It's the unwritten law of the land. And this is a full-time job. By the time you get one all fixed you have to start on the next one.

I well remember when Bill built our present cattle chute. That was awhile ago and it's just about worn out but oh what a joy when it was new. Our old one was dreadful and caused a great deal of grief. It created more excitement than would a Second Coming and many's the time I wanted to commit murder – to both men and beasts.

There's something about loading cattle: the men cannot seem to load even one calf without shouting to their wives to assist. I'm sure it's not togetherness which prompts this. Possibly it gives the husband someone to cuss at instead of the hired man – he might quit!

Anyway with the first call to duty, I'd be off and running. There was never time to change so I could be clad in anything from a cotton skirt to PJs as I grabbed my broom, ready for whatever.

My job was to crawl up the side of the stock rack and prod a poky critter into moving a bit faster. This takes some doing at times for you have to hang on with one hand and beat with the other. The odd time I'd land in the muck on the ground with Bill shouting over the edge, "Hey, what are you doing down there? Come on up and help!"

Once in a while some little thing like my skirt flipping or my whistling would startle one just coming up the chute, which would back down over Bill or who ever happened to be behind and they'd have to start all over again. By the time the cattle were loaded we humans were ready to collapse.

With the new chute it was a piece of cake. As it was built I remember thinking it seemed big – awful big! After Bill pounded in each six-inch spike he stopped to gaze at the chute. It was so massive we could load an elephant and it wouldn't budge.

There was a little walk along the edge for me so I wouldn't be in danger of falling off. And a neat little gate at the bottom so I could rip in and up the chute if need be to slam down the tail gate.

But there was one worry. They built that gate for a right-handed woman and I am a lefty. So I was sure I'd still have to crawl up and over and the thing was 12 feet in the air.

When Bill was off elsewhere I'd go out, worrying, to size it up. A trial run at it once caught me halfway up the side just as the neighbors and their had friends from England came by to visit. It took a bit of fast talking when they asked what I was doing. Try explaining why a sane woman is crawling up the side of a loading chute when there's not a truck, man or animal in sight!

Oh well, that's what makes farm wives unique.

Color Party

❀ ❀ ❀ ❀ ❀ ❀

Last summer I tried something new – a color party. Now I'm not into parties like these as I feel honor bound to buy something if invited. Also, I feel if I go to one for one friend, I should accept all invitations. So to keep things sane, I just refuse any invitations to these types of entertainment.

But this one was different. My one and only daughter-in-law was putting it on to help a friend and all my daughters, a granddaughter and a friend were to attend. So I thought it would be fun and give me a chance to visit my kids. Besides, I like make-up and nice clothes and I might just pick up a tip or two.

I realize women have been having their colors done for years. For me it was something new. For one thing, I wear whatever color turns me on, is on sale and is clean at the moment.

As I got ready I wondered, what do you wear to such an event? I picked out a pants outfit which boasted more colors than Joseph's coat, figuring I was bound to hit it right with at least one of these shades – regardless if I was a summer or a winter!

When I arrived I met the color lady and let me tell you, she was certainly put together – perfect hair, teeth, dress, shoes – even coat. Of course I might have been a mite envious. I had been cutting grass all day and had a great scrape down my arm where I had misjudged the space between trees. My hair was sticking every which way, besides which I had a dilly of a windburn on my face. So I was feeling more than a little vulnerable.

As she set up her mirror and got all her materials and make-up out, I sat back and relaxed for the first time that day. This get-together was going to revive me, I figured.

But I figured wrong. This lady meant business. She was dead serious. There would be no frivolous chatter this evening.

Orders started flying. "Who shall be first?" Nary a smile on her face. She even enunciated properly.

Well, there was no way I was going first – I'm not that brave. So Marcie, my granddaughter, was chosen. She was easy, she's a lovely little creature and as swatches were laid over her shoulders each one looked wonderful.

As all this went on I started joking with the girls and was told to pay attention. I gathered, rather shamefacedly, we were not to chat. We were to watch and state whether the swatch of material looked good on the girl or not.

Halfway through she ordered Kelly, my daughter-in-law, to get a towel to cover her hair. The "her" was me.

Heavens, I didn't think my hair was that bad! Apparently it was the color that was the problem.

"What is your *natural* shade?" I was asked, distaste emanating from the woman's perfect pores.

"Oh, reddish-brown," I answered.

"Well, that certainly does nothing for you."

By this time I was feeling a bit of a wreck.

"God knows your true color!" she stated but I couldn't figure out just what it had to do with God. I didn't worry about my hair, why should He?

She wasn't finished with me yet. It seemed a lot like "pick on Bets" day. I was ordered to go to the bathroom and remove ALL that make-up. So I trotted off like a good little girl and wiped away. What the perfect creature didn't seem to understand was, ALL the make-up was simply a red face due to windburn. When I returned, the burn glowing like the Eternal Flame, she frowned (perfectly of course) and said, "It must be imbedded!"

By this time I felt my Irish blood rising to a dangerous level. Not wanting to say, "Stuff it, lady!" and embarrass Kelly, I held back.

When my turn came, she laid swatches over my shoulders, asking the girls what they thought. With each movement she made with her perfect hands, she always seemed to ensure her perfect manicure showed in all its perfection. Here again, I might have been paranoid as I had just broken my last long nail scraping gum off the floor and my one thumb nail was black from where I had hit it when nailing the trellises up on the verandah.

I chatted a bit, had a glass of juice and left, holding back the urge to give her a good kick in the butt as I passed.

The evening must have been hard on her as well. We persisted in whispering and now and then the odd chuckle could be heard although these were met with a frown – perfect of course.

As I thought it over the next day I figured that lady needed some loosening-up pills. She should have at least tried to smile – after all she was collecting $20 from each of us.

On the other hand, I must have seemed a total enigma to her. I did not give her the adulation she felt she warranted. I tend to take other things far more seriously. The starving in underdeveloped countries, my children's future, my God and country – these frivolous things – above the seriousness of color co-ordinating! Probably shivers went up her perfect backbone when I said, "I'm not really too co-ordinated."

I tend to agree with Kathryn Hepburn, who stated, "When I started out as an actress I figured I could try to be on the Best Dressed list or I could go eccentric – I chose the latter and saved thousands of dollars!"

Anyway when all the chaff had blown away, I found I was a Summer with a bit of Spring thrown in and the colors she chose were basically what I had been wearing in one form or another for most of my life. So it wasn't a totally wasted evening.

I think I might try a lingerie party – that should be more fun!

Wrinkles

The other day I looked at myself in the mirror – a clean mirror which reflected back everything! Now that takes courage!

I realize a lot of people, especially teenagers, do a lot of mirror gazing each and every day. I don't. Oh, maybe way back when but certainly not for many years.

About four minutes a day is all – three to put on my makeup and one for whatever – getting a lash out of my eye, checking my hair length, or some other little thing.

Last night on TV there was a whole program on skin care, make-up and preventative measures to avoid wrinkles. Now I always use nice-smelling creams and moisturizers and "put on" my face each morning but I never thought too much about it. I use lotions and such to lubricate so I won't crack and make-up so I won't scare people. Wrinkles somehow really hadn't come to mind.

When I took this brave step and really looked at myself I was surprised – I didn't have wrinkles – I had gullies! How did this happen?

Gazing at myself in the mirror, I realized there was a reason for each wrinkle. Maybe if I eliminated the reasons, I'd prevent further damage. Of course I knew my age had a bit to do with it and I couldn't change that, however I thought it might be a good idea to try to prevent the ravines from deepening!

I started at the top. Forehead wrinkles – my there were a few of them. These were caused by frowning. How would I stop frowning? I frowned when things didn't go right, when I was trying to figure out how to fill out government forms, when I was trying to keep a premature baby calf alive on my kitchen floor and when I was trying to read my own handwriting. Well, there was no way I could ever stop frowning so those lines are there to stay.

Next, I went down to the lines around my eyes. As I wrinkled them up to see which muscles controlled that area, I realized they were "laugh lines" and every time I found humor in something, grinned, smiled or said hello to a dear one, read a funny story or saw a cute kid, these lines crinkled up like magic. I couldn't imagine trying to contain myself enough so these lines didn't appear.

Goodness, I wasn't having much luck. I went on down and found a deep wrinkle on one cheek. This had me buffaloed for a moment. What was this one caused by? I scrinched and scrunched like an idiot but couldn't find the movement that caused this one. Then it hit me. This was formed by lying on that side at night and the cheek was squished in that position. Well, to heck with that – I wasn't about to stay awake just to avoid that wrinkle!

Next I came to my mouth. I noticed many, very many, fine wrinkles all around my mouth, top and bottom. I had seen them before on grouchy people who purse their lips all the time but this wasn't what caused mine. I soon figured it out, though. I'm an addicted whistler. I whistle all the time, wherever I am. In fact my kids can locate me in a shopping mall by listening for the whistle. I knew there was no power on God's green earth that could stop me whistling – besides, I read a while ago if you want full, kissable lips, you should whistle. Mine are mighty kissable, but you just might fall in the wrinkles trying them out!

Neck wrinkles. These are caused by parts of me settling. I have a mole on my left cheek and was looking for it the other day when I finally found it under my chin!

When I finished looking for wrinkles, I sat back and assessed the situation. It didn't look too promising. If I was wealthy there were facelifts, so for fun I pulled my face back, folding all the loose skin over my hairline.

"So that's how I would look with a facelift!" It was certainly a nice smooth face, the wrinkles all ironed out and I found only one chin but something bothered me. I looked so bland – so empty! No character at all! I didn't like what I saw. So I let everything settle back, rubbed some nice smelling cream on and relaxed.

I realized I had earned every single wrinkle I had. These weren't wrinkles – they were character lines!

Oh, I might try again in a year or so. For now I'll just carry on, frowning, grinning, and whistling – besides, if I eliminated all the lines, I'd be so gorgeous I'd probably have to beat the men off with a stick and I haven't that much energy!

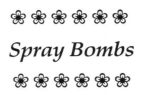

Spray Bombs

❀ ❀ ❀ ❀ ❀ ❀

Spray bombs – what on earth did people do before they came on the market? We've been led to believe you cannot have a clean house, a clean car or a good sex life without a few good aids such as these. Hair spray, oven cleaner – the list is endless; even whipped topping bombs for heaven's sake!

Whether we admit it or not, our forebears did manage quite effectively without them. Ammonia and water was a regular standby when it came to cleaning and disinfecting. This mixture worked two miracles: it cleaned everything it touched and the fumes killed any bugs within 15 yards. It only cost a pittance but then the manufacturers didn't have to pay for all the TV commercials we are forced to watch today.

The top of the old cook stove was kept shining like a new penny simply by rubbing it vigorously with a brown paper bag and the top was left clean enough to bake scones on it each Saturday.

Lemon oil and elbow grease were used on the furniture along with a good scrubbing with soapy water at spring cleaning time. Fly coils were strung up in each room to keep flies away and these proved quite effective. The odd time a human head got caught but coils were cheap and were changed whenever they were full of dead bodies.

There were fly swatters, though, which served a double purpose. Besides getting the flies, they kept the kids amused. Today kids watch TV – back then they were handed the swatter and told to get flies. A penny for two flies, a dime for spiders. This hard-earned cash bought jawbreakers in town.

Instead of all those glorious room fresheners available today, they tossed a sack of chloride of lime down the outdoor toilet and scrubbed the rest with lye soap every Saturday. Usually you were afraid to sit down until about Wednesday in case you got a burn!

Shaving cream – some had mugs and the men would rub their shaving brushes in these to whip up a good lather. I remember one old cowboy who used a bar of Lifebuoy soap and scraped the suds off with his jack knife.

There are so many rug cleaners and spot removers today and these we need. Back then, the rugs were small scattered ones made out of old rags which could be washed. The odd 9 X 12 would be hung out on the clothesline and beaten to death.

Toilets didn't plug up in the old West. Even if you had an indoor one, the old-time plumbers used such big pipes you could flush a cat down them without plugging up.

Grandma didn't need wood panel cleaners. She calcomined the walls and when she saved up enough egg money she'd paper them. The outdoor biffy was decorated with pictures from magazines she got from the old country. Wherever your eye rested was a different scene, either of an old English garden or a Highland cow.

Yes, they managed fine without those bombs. I do use bombs and I'm usually quite glad to have them but you have to be careful. One day, in a tizzy, I grabbed my hair spray and gave my head a good shot. It smelled funny. On second look, I just about flipped – my head was covered with oven cleaner!

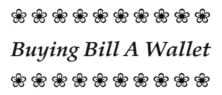

Buying Bill A Wallet

I did it – I really did it – I accomplished the task. I talked Bill into accepting a nice new wallet.

You can't honestly appreciate this amazing accomplishment without hearing a bit of background.

For more years than I can remember, he has carried the same old wallet about. There may have been a day when it was quite presentable, maybe even elegant but those days are long past.

That wallet was quite a sight, all out of shape, the stitching ripped here and there, the pockets for licenses and cards nowhere in sight, so that all the cards were tucked into the bill compartment. This didn't crowd anything too much, farming being what it is but the cards looked tattered and the whole thing resembled a mouse nest.

Every time he retrieved it from his front pocket to pay someone, little bits of silage and straw, along with the odd moth wing, sifted to the floor. Of course the fact that I had run it through the washer a few times didn't improve the overall look, either.

Now you are probably wondering why on earth Bill didn't get a new wallet. Well, he seemed strangely attached to this apparition – so much so that I wondered if he would stay as attached to me as time went on. I had given him a good seven new wallets over the years, only to have them given away or left lying forlornly in his sock drawer.

I remember his mother watching him pull the battered creature out of his pocket in church many years ago. Feeling he might bring shame on the Kilgour name, she went out and bought him an elegant one, with no luck.

He had variety, goodness knows. Black ones, brown ones, tooled leather, kangaroo skin; each one was met with the same stolid skepticism. One was too thick, one too thin, another too narrow. But the biggest excuse was always, "I've got a perfectly good one now!"

Soon his own children were old enough to try, so for every conceivable occasion he would get yet another wallet. When the kids looked aghast as he pulled the old thing out, he'd pretend it was the one he got from them. "Yeh, they just don't make them to last nowadays!"

Finally, I made a special trip to Red Deer to shop for the "impossible." A wallet not too thick, too thin, too narrow, too fancy or too plain which would replace that treasure he carried around. It took a day but I did it. Wrapped it up and went home. Made a special supper of roast beef and apple pie and asked him to take me to the picture show. Then, when he was having his bath, I burned the old one and laid the gift on his dress pants. There was a bit of a scene but it was well worth it!

P.S. With all those wallets in his drawer, I've got Christmas gifts for years!

New Babies

❀ ❀ ❀ ❀ ❀ ❀

First babies are such an experiment. Neither the baby nor the mother know the rules and there are no practice sessions ahead of time. Oh it would be nice if this whole thing could be like driving lessons with a test at the end but by the time you get the hang of it the kid is 20 years old!

Conception heralds not only the beginning of the baby but also the beginning of the whole experiment. And the minute you phone your mom, grandmother, or mother-in-law with the great news, you are greeted with, "Sit down, elevate your feet and find your pulse – I'll be right up!"

When my first baby was on the way, all aunts, grandmothers, great-grandmothers and even an uncle or two related to the little dot in the womb, started coaching.

The first thing I had to do was buy about 100 balls of white baby yarn and start knitting. It was as important as drinking milk! I must not buy blue or pink because I didn't know the sex of the baby and no one would ever dress a baby in any other color. It wasn't the British thing to do!

While I was to knit like crazy every time I sat down, I must NEVER let anyone see what I was knitting! This was not proper! If someone wandered in, I was to immediately hide the knitting under the couch and grab a sock to darn!

Besides knitting sweaters, booties and bonnets by the dozen, I also had to sew flannelette nighties. These garments were easy to make, with raglan sleeves and no collar. They had to be about a foot longer than the baby, I guess to get in the way and always be soaking. They also had to be embroidered all around the neck with tiny nosegays of pastel flowers in the finest of stitches, to look as good on the inside as out. No one informed me how to get the food stains out of them as time progressed.

I also had to make dozens of little white matinee jackets – also embroidered, pillowcases – also embroidered and some squares to carry the kid in – also embroidered. I had babies who had embroidery patterns embossed on their cheeks for six months from sleeping on all the embroidery!

It was a sort of unwritten law for all motherhood – to show your love, talent and imbecility, you must embroider!

Another fad back then was the binder. This was a piece of flannel about four inches wide which you wound around the baby's stomach to keep the belly button in place – if you neglected this, the child would most certainly become the victim of a hernia. I balked at this. After my baby arrived the first thing anyone checked on was the kid's tummy, hoping against hope he was suffering from a foot-long hernia!

Then I had to hem diapers – no disposables back then. By the time all that knitting and sewing is done and after having to go through doors sideways, you are looking forward to giving birth. You don't care if it's a football – you just want it out of there!

But that's when you find the real anxiety begins!

Regardless of the fact that you've read 14 books on Proper Parenting, five on Childcare, and a couple on Childhood Diseases, you are still paranoid. All of a sudden this bundle of joy is an awesome responsibility. Before, you were the most laid-back person in the country with a wealth of common sense, now you are a quivering wreck. You find yourself phoning the doctor with weird questions.

"I'm sorry to bother you, doctor, but I'm sure Jamie is ill. He drank only three to four ounces of his milk and when I forced the rest down his throat, he actually threw up!"

And mothers get phoned a lot.

"Mom, I know he's got sleeping sickness. He slept six hours straight!" or "Mom, I know he's got bladder infection. He wet fourteen diapers today!"

Your paranoia is even worse if you happen to be a nurse.

Along with the first baby come a multitude of friends and relatives loaded down with helpful hints, all feeling honor-bound to help you raise your kid. You soon come to realize there are twenty ways to do everything, each one different than the way you've been doing it.

But you sink or swim and common sense does come to the fore. You learn to merely smile with each hint and let it sift right on through. You also realize wee Jamie is not nearly as fragile as you thought. After all, it stands to reason if the kid can down three bowls of food at one blow and sleep eight hours through the night, there really can't be much wrong with him.

You learn you can lift him by the heels to change him without dislocating his hip joints and if he upchucks down your back the only real worry you have is getting the stain out of your blouse.

The next big step is learning not to compare kids. If you don't learn this, you'll go absolutely nuts. This can be especially trying if there are three or four other babies about the same age in your circle of friends. You'll learn not to panic when a mother states, "Bobby is crawling up and down stairs now – how is poor Jamie doing – still lying about?"

Try to answer such statements with a question like, "How many times did you let him fall on his head while he was accomplishing such a clever act at six months of age?"

Then there's the teething. You'll find yourself opening his jaws ten times a day and feeling about. By the time you've convinced yourself that you are raising the "toothless wonder of the century" he'll up and pop four in a week.

Another funny thing about first babies – you'll take 40 pictures a day. Pictures of him eating, sleeping, hiccuping and barfing. By the end of the first year, you'll have worn out your camera and by the time he goes to school, you'll have had to build on an extra room just to keep the albums in. Funny thing though, by your fifth child, the first pictures ever taken will be the grade one school photo!

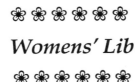

Womens' Lib

Through the years I've wondered about many things, one being Women's Liberation.

I have always believed in equal pay for equal work. I believe in equality, not only for women, for all people. I hate to see any person abused.

In fact, I think I was liberated even before the term became so popular and when I felt I wasn't, I changed things on my own.

What I don't like about the Women's Lib movement is the furore they seem to enjoy. The fuss, the placards held high in marcher's hands. The burning of bras! There is no way I will ever burn my bras – not at thirty bucks a shot!

No, I won't join the group, with good reason. I'd lose some things which I thoroughly enjoy.

Let me explain. As a farm woman, I'd be downright dumb to follow the Women's Lib movement. If we were equal to our men, we would have to "plough the fields and scatter" right along with them and then after a hard day in the field, we'd have to come in and make supper! That is not equality in my book.

This type of equality is fine in a pinch. In fact, it's fun to sit on the tractor and drive the truck when needed but not all the time.

Besides, we'd have to haul the silage, pack the bales, and even clean the corrals – whew! If this means equality, then I'm not for it.

And since when did I want to get up at 5:30 to feed the heifers and clean the stock tanks just to ensure I was equal to my husband?

No way. I enjoy staying in my nightshirt until the men leave the house. I enjoy having a second cup of coffee, even if it means getting the short end of the deal and being crushed asunder by the male population.

And think about this: I'd be equally responsible for all farm expenses. The gas and fertilizer bills, the land and machinery payments! Then I'd have to help with spraying, haying and harvesting, besides keeping the summer fallow up!

I know I'll be branded a traitor to the "Cause" when I say I'd much rather slip into my pink slacks and perfume and take some lemonade out to the men. Besides, I look a lot sexier in my pink slacks than my overalls. Although I've been told it's demeaning to look sexy!

Now if this equality is really working as it should, Bill would have to do his share of housework too – baking, scrubbing and ironing. Well, I don't know about you but I don't want any six-foot, greasy, overalled equal punching *my* bread down!

The dishes? Maybe. The ironing? The iron hasn't been scraped clean from the last attempt. And washing? Heaven forbid. One white undershirt, a pair of blue jeans, two soft pink towels and a greasy old jacket with a new red hanky in the pocket turned the last load a sickly pink!

Of course, I'd have to let Bill get the groceries, as well. Actually, we usually get the groceries together now but I pick the stuff out with good reason – his one try recently provided me with 20 pounds of Scotch oatmeal, four big leeks and a blood sausage for a treat! No, I like it the way it is: I pick out the groceries and he pays for them.

As far as the farming goes, if it depended on me working hand-in-hand with Bill and shouldering half of all responsibilities, we'd either go broke in a year or we'd commit murder or mayhem.

I can just hear the militants groaning in absolute disgust. Nonetheless, I rather like my lifestyle. I feel Bill and I are partners, each doing what we do best and respecting the other. I like to have doors opened for me and boxes carried. I also like the idea of the man picking up the tab at a restaurant. I even enjoy being patted on the head and called, "little girl," patronizing though it might be.

As far as marching with placards, I think Bill would just hand me two chop pails and send me to the bull corral on the way home from the rally.

No, I'm as liberated as I want to be right now. I rather like the pedestal I'm on and would be quite foolish to come off it, so I'll just have to remain a traitor to the Liberation movement. But I have a gut feeling most of these ladies will one day realize they lost something very special in their forward movement.

Toy Assembly is Child's Play?

❀ ❀ ❀ ❀ ❀ ❀ ❀ ❀

How many people are there in the world who have difficulty assembling toys and gadgets which come through the mail in five thousand funny-shaped pieces?

I know I have trouble with such things and I'm sure I'm not alone. Everything should come already together even if it takes a boxcar to carry it. For one thing, most of these things come with instructions meant only for an assembly line to follow and some are even in a foreign tongue.

First you have to find the proper tools and that, alone, can finish off the average farm wife. I head out to the shed and find that all the tools are off in the field somewhere. So it's resort to two screwdrivers with cracked handles, both the wrong size and a kitchen knife.

Now screw "this" into "that" and tighten the screws. But "this" doesn't fit "that," so I try "that" into "the other." At last I'm off and away or so I think.

Except that when I get it half together, it looks like a pregnant elephant. Take it all apart and start once more. Then there's more grief because I've tightened the screws so well the stem cracks and I beat the toy against the sink, trying to loosen the screws.

This sort of performance tends to leave one just a bit uptight. I quell the urge to chuck the whole gizmo out the door because it cost good money and the birthday is tomorrow. I have to get it together.

This time, parts that didn't fit seem to slide into place. The whole thing takes on its proper shape. There's only one problem. I've seven pieces left over! Besides, the wheel that's supposed to go around won't budge.

Apart it comes again. By this time I'm tempted to run into town and buy some little plastic toy for double the price but an empty wallet keeps me at it.

After five more tries, I stomp out of the room and have a hot cup of tea. The whole thing has turned into a mighty challenge, so I try once more.

If life were fair and each piece fit, you'd be done in 10 minutes. Fairness has little to do with it and "A" does not fit into "B." "G" is nowhere in sight and I've been at it for two hours.

Then Bill walks in. I turn and yell at him to remove his boots. Not that my dilemma has anything to do with his boots but all you women will understand you have to scream at *someone* at such times.

Soon, he's joined me and we're reading and fiddling with all the pieces. Two heads are better than one. Still we have trouble. Then along comes a neighbor and joins us. After another hour of screwing and unscrewing, we achieve what I had set out to do. Guess what – two hours after the kid gets this gift, he has it all apart on his bedroom floor! I hope he's cleverer than his parents because I'm not putting it together again!

New Home?
No Thank You!

Many friends and relatives have, at one time or another, tried to get Bill and I into a new house. To little avail, I might add.

I can understand their concern. The place I call home was built in 1914 by Bill's father, nine years after he settled on his homestead. Ever since then, it's had Kilgours living in it and I sincerely hope this trend will continue.

It's a treasure to me. I'm proud of its heritage and the way it stands loftily on the land. Granted it's been through a lot. Two generations have been reared there with a third enjoying the rooms every chance they get.

The first generation left nicks in the woodwork which are quite evident. I've had to replace the broken bricks in the fireplace where little Billy cut loose with his hammer! We've replaced most of the windows but the robins and swallows still nest by the front door.

Our children left their marks as well. The bannister doubled as a slide so many times over the years, the bottom post has moved ahead a good three inches. The plaster on the kitchen wall hung precariously for years after a stray ball bounced off it during a fun-filled afternoon. The upstairs floor jounces a little and if you look, you just might find some initials carved in unique spots.

I think our hesitancy over the years is because we are not "new house" people. New houses tend to scare me. They seem so austere and perfect. I think I'd be uneasy living in one. They seem so neat and unused. One thing about this place – there's not a corner which is not utilized, it's the most lived-in place in the country. It's homey!

Oh, through the years, we've changed things some. The plaster has been papered over and we keep the walls, inside and out, painted up.

At one time when the kids were all home, I thought I would like a great big utility room on the back. I could have double sinks for the men to wash in, as well as a great closet for the chore clothes and boots. The fridge, washer and dryer as well as the deep freeze would all be moved out there. It sounded just lovely!

As you know, one doesn't get everything one wants in this world. On a farm your first priorities are the things that pay for themselves, like a bull and six heifers, the machinery and seed. So my dream dissipated as we built the farm, raised the kids and tried to keep our heads above water. The dumb thing is, even if I could get that utility room now, I'd say, "No thank you!" I'm content the way things are. I was always content in this house and as our family grew and more memories were overlaid, our home became even more precious.

All the stuff we have accumulated over the years, which would be out of place in a modern home, somehow fit perfectly into our rooms. Reminds me of an old Duchess down on her luck, sitting proudly on the land from whence she sprang.

There's a quote: "When you get older, you realize all the things you wanted as a youth, you don't want any more!" which hit me dead centre – it's not the plaster and wood, it's the life lived in a house that counts and oh, we have wonderful memories. All the joy, the love, the pain and pleasure are woven into the whole atmosphere of this home. That can never be replaced.

We'll be happy for friends in new homes and enjoy our visits but it's so nice to come home to Crocus Coulee!

❀ ❀ ❀ ❀ ❀ ❀ ❀ ❀ ❀ ❀

The Farmer's Wife

❀ ❀ ❀ ❀ ❀ ❀ ❀ ❀ ❀ ❀

Homemaking Boring?
Heavens No!

I read somewhere that to be "just a housewife" is boring and boredom rots the soul. Boring? I'm "just a housewife" and I sometimes wish it were not quite so exciting!

Now don't get me wrong – I'm not against working mothers or any such thing and every woman, housewife or not, needs an outlet – some part of her life only for her. It doesn't matter what it is – hang gliding or raising chickens. Work of any kind can be boring at times if you let it but homemaking boring? Wow!

The main reason I don't find it boring is because of the unexpected. You can get up at six and plan an ordinary, (hopefully) productive day. By ten past eight, your plans are shot. You know what I mean - the porridge boils over on the cat, one of the kids has lost a shoe, meanwhile the school bus is tooting away in the yard. You locate the shoe in the bread box, kick the cat down to the basement and find the lunches still on the counter. Racing like mad to catch the school bus, housecoat flapping, you toss the lunches through a bus window as it backs up and in so doing, pop the second last button off your housecoat.

Back in the house you settle down for the first sip of coffee you've had all morning, hoping for boredom to set in.

"I'll dust, vacuum and possibly do a bit of baking." Just as you plug in the vacuum a neighbor phones wondering if you know your cattle are out and running down the highway. Shunning the idea of possibly going into hibernation, you hurry off to find the farmer in your life.

If life were fair and all, he'd be coming up the walk with a smile on his face but no luck. You finally track him down on the south quarter under a tractor with 17 odd parts spread on the ground around him.

Of course, he's delighted with your tidings of great joy. That's why he tosses a wrench forty yards and cusses at the dog.

Before boredom has a chance to set in, you find yourself chasing an assortment of four-legged creatures all over hell's half acre. As you try to get them through the gate by which they escaped, the cattle decide they would rather play little games like "through the thistles we shall dance!" and are not inclined to lope into a dreary, old corral, so it's nigh on high noon by the time you're back in your kitchen.

After dinner you try once more to relax and be bored with ironing, baking and dusting. Before you even plug the iron in, a salesman drives up and by the time you can get to the door, your Irish Setter has a chunk of pants in his mouth and the poor man is yelling bloody murder.

After assuring him your dog is not rabid or hungry, you settle the fellow down with strong coffee and end up buying four bottles of tonic to ensure you won't be sued.

From that moment on there are phone calls, visitors, and runs in to town for parts. You poke a casserole in the oven and sit down with your feet up, hyperventilating. Even then, you are interrupted with a phone call – 4H tonight, they need a square and you are on devotions at the Guild meeting next day.

At twelve that night you brush your teeth, wash up and pray fervently that tomorrow will truly be a mite boring, even if your soul does rot a little!

Saskatoon Picking

❀ ❀ ❀ ❀ ❀ ❀ ❀ ❀ ❀

Each and every spring I wait for the saskatoon bushes to bloom; wait with baited breath, praying no frost, drought or other natural disaster will hit before the berries are ripe and waiting to be picked.

In early times the western prairies were a regular larder of foodstuffs. Wooded areas were filled with wild game of all sorts; deer, elk and moose; the streams and rivers teemed with fish and the shorelines were home to much wild fowl.

There were also many native fruits. The one which stood the test of time is the "lowly" saskatoon berry. Actually, it's a delicious and versatile fruit.

The Indians beat it into their pemmican for added flavor and when the settlers arrived they soon learned what a boon it was to their food shelves. Every July found pioneer women and kids out in the saskatoon patch picking by the hour. Each fall their cellars and fruit cupboards held hundreds of jars of saskatoon preserves, jams and jellies. This, along with dried fruits and rhubarb made up desserts for the long winter months.

To this date, saskatoon bushes can be found in the draws and coulees and riverbanks of the prairies.

I remember the first time I went saskatoon picking with Bill. We had only been married a wee while and although I had picked cranberries and blueberries as a kid, I wouldn't have known a saskatoon bush from a palm tree. However, I was good at bluffing.

I was still in the "always look sexy for your man" mode and also felt we might do little actual picking so I donned (I was still young enough to don clothes, now I just get dressed) a pair of white slacks and leather sandals which had set me back three months' wages. With a shot of cologne, I was set for whatever.

Hoping these elusive berries would be on nice bushes about waist high and near the road, I soon got a rude awakening. They were on the side of a blooming gully! With a merry, "Come on, honey!" Bill grabbed my hand and off I went, slithering and sliding away. "You take that bush and I'll take those over on the edge!"

Not wanting to appear a sissy, I said, "When I'm finished, I'll come help you!" and started in picking the things.

I worked like an idiot, wanting to pick more than Bill. But I had a lot of grief. I had brought only a small pail without a decent handle and wouldn't let Bill tie a string on it because "It might mess my hair!" So I could only pick with one hand. The mosquitoes were out in full force, drawn to my perfume possibly and ants were working their way through the straps of my sandals. My slacks were purple where I had wiped my hands and my head was aching.

By the time an hour was up Bill was finished. I was too but not in the same manner. His bucket was full and he was whistling away. He came by, pulled me back up the hill and showed my his handiwork. The bucket was full of lovely, rich, uniform berries. There wasn't a leaf or a twig to mar the perfection.

Then I showed him my effort and he had the audacity to laugh! Quelling the urge to empty it over his head, I instead looked carefully inside my bucket. Heavens, it was only half full and held more leaves and twigs than berries. The berries were a sad lot, some wrinkled, some green. An orange worm reclined on the top.

Even so, I took them all home, made some pies and was hooked for life. I became a berry-picking junkie. Of course my attire changed dramatically. After all, I might be a little dull but I'm a fast learner. An old long-sleeved shirt of Bill's and jeans replaced white slacks and my sandals have been switched for boots. I still use perfume but it's mixed with mosquito repellent.

My kids all had their turn in the berry patch – some willingly and some not; even some of them are now addicted. Heavens, I have grandchildren now coming with me so I'm an actual matriarch of a berry-picking dynasty!

Cleaning Out the Fridge

Three cheers and a big hurrah – I cleaned out the fridge today. I'm now out to turn cartwheels on the lawn with a glass of wine in my hand.

Three quarters of you will understand my jubilation. It takes courage to clean a fridge.

For one thing you've been stashing away three peas, four beans, a dab of stew and half a wiener for how long? This is so easily done. You are busy with harvest, silage, Christmas – whatever and the easiest thing to do is chuck it in there. But the time had come to do something. Not being wealthy, I couldn't buy a new fridge and take the poor sick one to the dump – a thought that did pass my mind. Besides the thing was emitting strange smells, so bad that when I opened the door the dog got up and wanted out.

The door was also giving me a bit of worry as it was taking on a shape of its own and curves even Dolly would be jealous of. I don't think the hinges could take another day it was so stuffed.

It's strange how women are prone to storing all sorts of bits and pieces in the fridge, knowing full well in their subconscious they will never use them up. Why we don't just throw these bits away in the first place, I'll never know. I know I can't. Maybe it's the old pioneer instinct in me or something. If I throw as much as a kernel of corn out, I have nightmares of starving African babies gazing at me with soulful eyes.

Strange thing is I can toss away three quarters of the same stuff two months later with nary a quiver of guilt. I imagine the reason for this nonchalance is because not a living soul would eat it by then.

I find the best time to clean out the fridge is on a bad day. It helps to be in a nasty mood. If you're not, you're bound to be by the time you're finished anyway, so why spoil a good day?

First, unplug the machine. From there, you know the routine – jab away at the ice, scrape off the Freezie label and pop the hair dryer in full blow.

Then start on the bottom section. My, my, what you don't find. Five dishes of grey something, a bowl with green fuzz on the top, a half a head of lettuce frozen stiff and one kippered herring stuck to a mitt.

Lay out anything that's remotely edible for a casserole and then proceed with great secrecy to dispose of the rest. I've tried flushing the gunk down the toilet but so much of it tends to float and cause great consternation to those next using the bathroom.

"Mom, there's something ALIVE in the toilet!!" Being married to a garbage can scrounger, I have to bury it well down in the ashes or it might just come back with instructions to not waste food. One time he came in with a half a rotten apple and told me with Highland superiority to be more selective. I put it in his lunch that day with a love note hoping he would think of me when he ate it.

Anyway, I scrubbed and rubbed, sprayed and polished and the fridge now looks lovely. I can see my shelves and find I have to quell the urge to leave the door open so I can gaze upon its pristine loveliness.

I vow to clean it once every three weeks from now on, but you know how it goes – three peas, a chunk of bread and a soup bone and here I go again!

Farm Women Can Do Anything!

One thing rural women have in common is versatility. We can be dressed to perfection, nails polished, hair in the latest style and sexy to boot one moment and in ten seconds be in our old chore clothes, knee deep in muck, helping where we're needed. This we have learned to handle with great speed and good grace as well as a huge sense of the ridiculous. Here's just one example of this transformation.

I was invited to give the opening talk at a Farm Women's Conference. I knew of and had taken part in these conferences before. They are held once a year for all farm women and are quite wonderful. You visit with your peers, listen to speakers of all kinds and go home rejuvenated.

In order to speak at 9:00 a.m., I had to be up early to help drive the silage truck. Then I ripped back in the house, chose my clothes carefully and spent more than my usual three minutes on my make-up, before packing up my props and projector.

I arrived in good time. The weather was perfect. After my talk, instead of coming home, I decided to stay for lunch. We were into calving but with the weather so pleasant, I figured I wouldn't be needed.

I enjoyed the time, listening to other speakers and picking up a few tips like, "Sure you can wear a belt even if you can't find your waistline."

After lunch I headed for home feeling refreshed. As I drove along I noticed dark clouds to the west and wondered if we were in for a skiff of snow and prayed fervently it wouldn't amount to much. Calving is enough work without dealing with wet snow. About three miles from home, the storm hit with a vengeance. The snow was swirling around so much I could barely see the road, so it was with great relief I finally turned into the lane. As I drove up, Bill met me.

"Bets, change quickly – we've got three new calves to bring in from the far end!"

So five seconds later I was tossing my good clothes unceremoniously on the bed and crawling into warm ones. Bill's old overalls finished my ensemble. I ran to the tractor, pulling on my toque and mitts as I went.

We headed across the bumpy pasture searching for the new babies and found we had five, not three, to bring in.

Bill hasn't much faith in my tractor driving experience, with good reason. I've upended him the odd time, so my job was to sit in the bucket of the front-end loader and hold the slippery wet calf while Bill backed us up to the corral. Of course this has to be done in slow motion so the worried Mommy will be able to keep smelling her baby. With each bawl from the calf, she figured I was molesting it and brought her horns precariously near me. But farm women aren't chicken – at least we never let on we are.

By the time the fifth baby and mother were safely in the barn, I was a soggy, wet creature with barely enough oomph to crawl to the house. As I peeled off, I took a peek in the mirror and couldn't help giggling.

Lord, I was a mess. What a change from the morning! Yes indeed, farm women can dress up or dress down. And I still believe I look just a mite sexy in Bill's overalls!

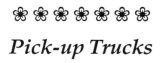

Pick-up Trucks

Along with a husband, five kids, ten grandchildren and an assortment of hired men and animals, I've also acquired the odd pick-up truck during my many years here at Crocus Coulee. It's usually been a battered, cantankerous one – partly due to me.

Now I can toss up a great salad, turn a meal out for 15 in 20 minutes and raise great kids; I'm also a very loving wife and don't fuss when I have to pick up dirty underwear. Despite all this, pick-ups and I just don't get along.

I avoided driving them as long as possible but when the day came when we didn't own a car. I was forced to face the issue.

You can't imagine how happy I was when we got another car. Yet even to this day, I have to drive the pick-up at times. I'll have an appointment in town and Bill will be using the car or I'll want to get groceries and the car is being serviced or there's been a breakdown and I have to go for parts. As I head toward the pick-up I feel its baleful glare and can almost hear it muttering, "What's that dim-wit going to put me through today?"

I'm fine with big trucks. Oh there's the odd scratch or the odd smell of burnt rubber but I feel in control. But the pick-up? There's something inside me, beyond my control which causes me to hit, run over, bend, scrape and demolish everything in my way, front or back.

I'll be whistling down the road and the door flies open. I'll be trying to park sedately in front of the post office and the straw underneath will catch fire. I'll miss the brakes and hit the gas, running over a bike before I come to rest. Or I'll forget to signal and end up scaring the wits out of some poor driver just silly enough to believe I have all my faculties.

Backing up seems to be my nemesis. I remember Bill sending me for buckets of oil or whatever. This should have been simple. All I had to do was back up to the warehouse and stop close to the platform. I started backing in, praying fervently I had no onlookers. I thought I was straight but the owner shouted, "Better pull out and try again, you're at quite an angle." He should have left well enough alone. I eased out, came in at the right angle and clipped two old oil drums. Four times I tried and finally got backed up – but not before taking a foot long chunk out of the platform. By the time I was loaded I was weak with tension and the fellow was downing four aspirin.

Surely a truck with the same steering wheel, brakes, and gears as I've used for years would be a cinch to manage but I seem to be always ill at ease with it. Even if I don't damage the truck, I run over garbage barrels, hit fences, cause war veterans to faint.

We've got a pick-up now that is marvellous – Bill has a real love affair with it but this thing is so high up I have to run to get in it. I carry a stool with me because when I go to town with Bill it's downright embarrassing to be seen being hauled in like a beached whale by a grunting sweaty man.

I don't give up easily. Why just yesterday I made it all the way down the road four miles to check on the horses and only hit the ditch once, narrowly missing a deer!

A Good Healthy Lie Will Do

I adore a good liar! Really! Not that I don't know that lying is one of the Ten Commandment NO NOs. And I really don't indulge in lying myself. What I am talking about is just a mild pleasant lie. I hold a special warmth for the person who can stretch the truth just enough to make me feel good.

Not long ago I met an old friend who used to take me out the odd time before I met Bill. I recognized him immediately. When I spoke to him, he looked at me with such a blank face I felt like an idiot. When I introduced myself, he pulled through majestically.

"Why, Betty, it can't be you. You haven't changed a bit." Then to add more fuel to the fire he had lit in me, he finished off with, "You must have found the fountain of youth!"

Of course, it was all nonsense and he was just an old smoothy but wasn't that better than being told, "Boy, you're sure getting on, girl!"

I don't know why I'm so taken in by false compliments. It might possibly date back to my life as a kid. All the kids I went to school with were brutally honest. So honest, in fact, I still carry the mental bruises.

"Let Betty kick the ball, her feet are the biggest!"

"Let Betty play in Mike's place. She's shaped like a boy!"

I never once let on these remarks bothered me but when I was alone I'd lick my wounds by daydreaming. In these dreams I was the heroine and my hero would be slathering at my feet.

"Why Elizabeth, your eyes are as blue as Killarney's lakes!"

All my dreams took place in Ireland with Irish people in every scene. I probably figured the Irish were better liars than other folks.

But I'd always be brought back down to earth with a thump on the back by another honest remark. Now, as an adult, I enjoy a good hearty lie.

When I buy a new dress I want to be told, "You look lovely!" not something more truthful like, "It makes you look thick in the waist!"

And when I ask Bill how he wants his eggs cooked, I want to hear, "Why, any way at all my darling, as long as it's your little hands that cook them!" not "Gosh, do I have a choice?"

When I buy something special for someone I want it stressed, "Why it's absolutely perfect, thank you!" not "What the H___ is it?"

When I wear a new suit which I rather feel doesn't suit me and is identical to the one the old lady down the street has, I still want to hear, "My it's lovely – that suit brings out something within you!" I don't want to hear WHAT it brings out. I just want a good healthy lie.

Doctors are supposed to have good bedside manners but sometimes they, too, are brutally honest. When I go in with a bladder infection, I do not need to be told, "Take these pills every four hours and stay near the bathroom." I know all that. I want to hear something comforting, such as, "You have a nasty germ, however you are brave, healthy and a martyr. I know you will overcome!"

Someone may have once said, "Flattery is only skin deep." That's as deep as I want it. The truth is embedded down where my arthritis is starting and I know that already.

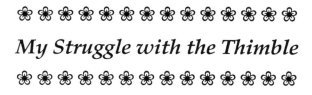

My Struggle with the Thimble

I was dusting my china cupboard the other day and un-earthed all sorts of interesting things, one being an old thimble.

Many girls today wouldn't have a clue what this strange little thing is. There's not likely a grandmother over sixty who hasn't seen one or used one or could sew a stitch without one.

In my old Home Economics days, our teacher tried valiantly to teach the finer art of using a thimble.

"If you are ever going to excel at sewing, you simply must use a thimble!" we were told. This was said in the same tone as if she had said, "If you are going to keep the baby alive, you must feed it!"

She had problems, though. Only one of the girls in the class *wanted* to sew in the first place, never mind excel at it. To the rest of us that thimble was a nuisance. We were clumsy enough without having an object on the end of a finger.

When the teacher wasn't scolding us, our mothers would be. We just wouldn't use one. I'm not sure why we balked – maybe peer pressure.

"Once you sew with a thimble, you'll love it and will sew much better!" our teacher enthused. It got to be a passion with the teachers. Thimble using fitted into the same category as being a good Liberal and of British stock.

We used to get thimbles for birthdays, Christmas and Eas-ter, along with our hankies. These thimbles were special, some with flowers on them, laid out on pink satin in a dainty box. I guess mothers thought we'd go for them if they were pretty. It didn't work.

I think the reason we were so stubborn was because we had been coaxed, cajoled and scolded so much we simply got our backs up. We used to hide them; every single one we got, pretty or not, mysteriously disappeared down the sugar bin, in an old pot or stuck in the soil of Mom's geraniums.

Mothers don't give up easily. Off they'd go to buy another. I felt sorry for the storekeeper. Each month he'd order flour, sugar, macaroni, and 100 thimbles. If they had been worth any great price, the fellow would have been a millionaire. They only cost seven cents a piece, so all it did was upset the man.

A neighbor lady who lived across the street noticed me sewing without a thimble and decided to accomplish what three Home Ec teachers and Mother could not.

"Now dear, just slip it on and push the needle through!" But I couldn't feel the needle and had no control over where it went. If I had only thought about it, the thimble would have been helpful – as it was I pushed the needle through with my finger so much I had open raw sores on it. The thimble would have prevented that. Finally, in desperation, the kindly lady came up with an offer she thought would have me using a thimble.

"Betty, if I buy you a lovely new piece of material, will you promise to use the thimble to sew it?"

It was such a kind thought and a very generous one in those tough times. I had to say "No thank you" and walk home. The last thing I wanted was another chunk of material to fight over with a thing that was so alien to me.

What this gesture did to me was hang a guilt trip so heavy on my shoulders, it took years to lift.

After Bill and I were married, his mother took over, knowing she could accomplish what others failed to do. She also lost the battle. Even though I was not using a thimble, I was nursing war wounds. I was shellshocked – I'd dream of being tied to a chair and forced to use a thimble. I was suffering the pains of the damned.

I was in my tenth year of marriage before I finally took a stand.

"I can't use a thimble, I don't want to use a thimble and I'm quite delighted to go down in disgrace!"

By this time I had fallen in disgrace some few times anyway. As I look back, the lack of a thimble didn't really cause me to flop as a seamstress – I sewed every stitch for four girls all the time they were at home and not once did they complain of the end product.

As I look at the thimble now, I have to chuckle. I try it on and it still feels horrid, so I toss it back in the sugar bowl and walk away laughing.

I'm Weird

❀ ❀ ❀ ❀ ❀

You know the longer I live the more I realize, I'm weird. I tend to look at things differently than most of our population.

I can't seem to go along with the adoration shown Hollywood stars just because the world deems them beautiful. Sure, they may possess a lovely form or beautiful legs or eyes but what does that prove? They didn't earn all that beauty – and in this day and age it's more than likely half plastic anyway. No, I tend to admire people who have accomplished something. Take Mother Theresa. She's no raving beauty but look what she has done for the poor and helpless. To me that's true beauty and success.

Even amongst ordinary humans, the trend is to admire things in others I just wonder about – but then I told you I think I'm a bit weird.

Tell me what is so great about getting up at 5 a.m. in order to get your wash finished by 8? Heavens, the woman has had three good hours to do it in! Nope, for me the real success story is the woman who gets *up* at 8, has two cups of coffee and has her wash finished off by 9:30. Or better yet, stayed in bed and talked someone else into doing it in the first place!

And what's so great about pulling out your stove and fridge twice a week just to scrub beneath them? Heavens, anyone can do that, all it takes is three good tugs and a bucket of soapy water. No, the one for me is the lady who can wash around these things for nine months and not have a soul notice the dust weevils!

And all those who get such high praise simply because their deep freeze is full of baking, when they have only one kid who just happens to be allergic to wheat flour – that's all fine and dandy. Take a look at the girl who has a hungry husband, six kids and two hired men – she actually broke her own track record and baked three cakes and four batches of cookies and managed to get half of them cooled and frozen before anyone got to them! She's the winner in my book!

It's awfully easy to scrub and wax your kitchen floor three times a week when you live in a small apartment in town. But what of the woman who lives on a hog farm, has three hired men, a growing family and actually keeps her back porch clean for a full day and not one soul stuck to her kitchen floor during harvest? Don't you think she has extra special talent?

And then the parents who sent their two boys off on a tour of Australia to broaden their education – sure they are to be commended but let's not forget that family out west who also had two sons. Instead of going to Australia they stayed home to help put up the hay for no pay other than a new pair of Levis and a young calf each after harvest – that also deserves special recognition.

There's always such a mark of distinction when someone builds a house 30 feet longer than the resident millionaire. What of the old folks, their parents, who still live in their first home, a two-bedroom model they built when first married? They, to me, are winners – they don't have any mortgage hanging over them and in many cases were the ones who made it possible for the young ones to live such a fine lifestyle!

And then there are those who proudly state, "I will never allow a fly in my home – all it takes is cleanliness!" Fine – especially if no one ever opens the door. But I stand up for the woman who lives surrounded by corrals and has an ongoing war with flies. She is able to clear the house and get them vacuumed off the window sill in the ten minutes she has after hearing the minister is heading out her way.

Now we should all gasp in awe when Jane shows us her Paris original which cost her a cool two thousand – but don't you think Kelly, who whipped up a cute little outfit out of a ten-dollar remnant and a second-hand zipper, has more talent?

All that noise about the lady who always has a clean oven – heck, it's clean because she never uses it and buys her pies at the bakery! Oh well, I guess anyone who can get away with buying her pastry does deserve a hand!

A Farm Woman's Routine

In so many of the glossy women's magazines today, they stress ROUTINE. You must follow a rigid routine. Then and only then will you be the perfect partner and this will lead to health, wealth, and happiness. But they forgot to give routine a good stiff road test on a busy farm! If they had, they would have quickly gone screeching back to the drawing board.

I know – I've checked some of these routines to see if they were feasible and there was no way I could work around them. First they state: Arise 8 a.m. Well fine but first of all a farm wife never ARISES! Instead, she *crawls* out of bed anywhere from 5 a.m. to 7 a.m.

Next, we are to "allow ourselves time to apply our make-up and stop another moment to meditate" Heavens! The only make-up we have on at five or six is what we forgot to remove the night before. As far as the meditation goes, that's the time we have to get five kids on the school bus, two men fed and sent to the field, and the meat taken out of the deep freeze. Then we sit down for a cup of extra strong coffee. Then and only then do we apply make-up although I'm not sure a shot of moisturizer and slap of lipstick in the bathroom really fits that description.

Now our morning really begins. You cannot keep a rigid routine on the farm because too many things can change your plans. If you say, "I'll vacuum and bake this morning, lunch will be leftovers and I can finish my ironing afterward," it all sounds quite wonderful and should be easy. Of course, the first thing that happens is an SOS from Bill.

"Please run in and get me one of these!" and he hands me a greasy machine part which just expired. So a quick run through with the comb and off I go. By the time I get the part, take it to the field and get back to my routine, close to an hour has passed – the time I planned to vacuum. "Oh well, I'll still get that cake made" and I did. When the lunch worked out, "Gee, maybe I'll get both the ironing and that vacuuming done!"

By 1:30 Bill is back with three guys who want to see the new bull. No discussion on any kind of bull can be enjoyed without coffee and the kitchen table to lean on. So there goes not only my ironing time but also the cake I just made.

Luckily, "never say die" is my motto and so I start up the vacuum only to run it back and forth three times when I'm needed.

"Hey Bets, the market's jumping – give us a hand to cut some steers out!"

By this time I give up on routine. It takes a good hour to cut the steers out, then time to find my scissors to cut off the ear tags. Then it's suppertime. I still have to make a square for the church bazaar and pick the beans.

By bedtime, I have come to my senses. "Lord, if you wanted me to have a routine you would not have placed me here on a farm. Oh and thank you for placing me on this farm – I couldn't hack all the rigidity stuff – AMEN!"

Repairmen

There is one relationship more important to women than any other – the relationship they have with their repairmen.

If you can honestly say, "What repairmen?" you're either living in a cave with bowls made of horn or at Buckingham Palace with nothing to worry about but keeping your nails up. Even there you'd need a telephone repairman now and then.

Ask any woman and she'll tell you, every blasted appliance she owns is going to give trouble at one time or another, sometimes two at the same time. It's Murphy's Law and these disasters always happen at the worst possible moment.

The washer: when it's rained for a week, the kids have school holidays, the men are cleaning the corral and you have 14 loads of laundry in various smelly piles.

The dishwasher: the day before Christmas with 30 guests expected.

The stove: on branding morning with the crew expected.

I'm not sure why this happens but I figure either God is teaching us patience or He has a comic sense of timing!

These are the reasons a farm wife develops her Love/Hate relationship with odd-looking men in overalls. Each wife has her own plan of action, as do I. I hit the phone with a vengeance, planning ahead what I'll say.

"Fred, this is Betty. My oven quit on me and I've ten men to feed!"

"Betty who?"

Oh, this is a toughie! I think.

"Betty, the one who makes you those delicious brownies!"

"I'm on a diet and can't come 'til Thursday."

"What about the ten men, Fred? I'm desperate!!"

"Just feed them the brownies."

Okay, so he wants to play nasty.

"Fred, I'm the Betty who has friends in high places, especially those who issue business licenses!" I realize this is a dirty way to deal but desperate times demand desperate actions.

Now you might be lucky and have a repairman with a great and compassionate nature and these you treat with gentleness and care bordering on the ridiculous.

"My dishwasher's broken and Kent's coming!" I yell to all within two miles. Then I hurry and scrub the kitchen floor – he mustn't get his jeans dusty when he crouches down. I lay out a clean white towel to set his tool box on – it must not get scratched! A fresh pot of coffee is on the go and I put on a dab of lipstick and cologne. Then I remember – oh no, he's the repairman with an allergy to perfume! It's the vacuum guy who likes Estee Lauder!

Each repairman is approached from a different angle. This takes several years to perfect. Here are four little rules you can safely follow:

1. Use flattery. "Your talent at fixing toaster reminds me of a brain surgeon!"

2. Beg. "I'm absolutely desperate!" in a tone which could signify murder, suicide or divorce.

3. Threats. Get downright dirty if the need be. "Bring it in??? Well, I heard of a woman who brought her motor in and she dropped in on the guy's foot, broke four bones, and he's still hobbling. What's your address?"

4. Bribe. "I'm so glad you have such a great reputation for promptness. I'll recommend you to 15 relatives, all with washers and a boatload of refugees!"

And when you actually find a repairman who is obliging and helpful, the sort who understands our dilemmas, hang on to him with a passion – treat him as a sheik with you in his harem. It will be well worth the fuss!

Flying Bathmats

❀ ❀ ❀ ❀ ❀ ❀ ❀ ❀

I'll bet I've got the only magical flying bathmat set in all the northern hemisphere. In fact I've got two sets and both spend more time flying through the air than decorating what they're supposed to.

Why, you ask? That's a good question. I appreciate stuff like bathmats and seat covers. They tend to hide what I want hidden. Bill has a pet aversion to these decorative creatures, as he has for anything that doesn't pay its own way and provide a necessary service.

He joined the navy at 17 and the old Royal Canadian Navy way of "spit and polish" has been ingrained in his very soul. Nothing out of place and everything stowed away neatly – except his stuff, of course (but that's another story).

All this fuss in the bathroom raises just enough of my Irish stubbornness to keep fighting back. The second he goes into the bathroom, I hurl myself down the hall behind him to catch the flying projectiles, either the mat or the seat cover. If I miss I find the object embedded in the wall. If I'm quick I can toss it back in at his feet, yelling all the while.

"Bill, I just washed that!"

"I've told you, Bets, they're bloody dangerous!"

"Oh did it attack you again?" I snarl.

"They are junk!" That's the end of this round.

He's still muttering five minutes later when he comes out. "They're a terrible waste of a man's money and besides, the lid won't stay up!"

"Hold the lid up with your other foot," I suggest with a grin as I imagine this exercise.

Now I'm not really mean to Bill. I've even bought special ones I thought he'd like, with sailors and boats on them – but out they went. I'm afraid to utter the ultimatum, "It's either me or the seat cover!"

But there's something good to be found in every trouble. I get some wonderful exercise chasing and catching those things. You're never sure of the angle they are going to fly out at and it's great for the reflexes. Reminds me a bit of clay bird shooting!

I'm not giving up. I think next time I go in there I'll whiz out his razor or his Tums. When he yells, I can counter, "There is no room for such frivolous things and besides, they are full of germs and don't match the wallpaper!"

If you someday view a woman sailing through the air on a bathmat, clutching a seat cover, it's really not extra-terrestrial. It's just me. Bill has finally sent me into orbit!

❀❀❀❀❀❀❀❀❀

Spring in Bloom

❀❀❀❀❀❀❀❀❀

Rain

It's funny how rain affects people differently.

To the city folk rain is practically a death warrant. All their weekend fun depends wholly on Mother Nature's whims.

I sometimes feel in a wet year every one of them would gladly gather together like Moses' people and melt every brass pot and kitchen sink to build an idol to worship, if it would just keep the rain away.

The golf game with the million dollar business deal tied in can be sealed or broken just by a lousy day. And heaven help the poor parents who promised their five kids a visit to the zoo and a picnic afterward, if a wet front moves in. No matter what they attempt to ease the grief, short of mass murder, it's still going to make the battle of Dunkirk look like a Sunday School picnic.

And now the powers that be have proven that rainy days cause depression. These days, depression is a horrifying word, something for which the government should authorize a commission study!

If the ladies plan a tea, its success hinges on the weather. I'm not sure why. I can sip a cup of tea on a rainy day as well as a sunny one. Possibly this dates back to the old buckboard days when you couldn't venture out if there was a much as a puff of cloud in the west. Even with our good cars and paved streets, women in the city hesitate to venture forth on a rainy day. Maybe their hair will straighten or their color run; anyway, they tend to stay home regardless of the cause they're supporting.

Rain is a pain to the city people and I can understand this. To the farmer it's a different thing. It's spelled GLORY in capital letters.

In the city rain arrives in showers, downpours and miserable all-day rains; to the farmer it comes in two-tenths, five-tenth and that million-dollar rain!

The men go hairy and the women try to keep the porch door shut. The kids are happy 'cause Dad and Mom are so content, they bask in whatever is causing this joy. The heavier the rain the happier the family. For on this rain hinges next year's taxes, the new bull, clothes, even a new paring knife.

If the rain begins at night the men run out to the rain gauge in their shorts and rubber boots at 6 a.m. to see how much has fallen already. Then they phone their neighbor one-half mile away to see how much he got!

"Boy, John, it's a dandy – I've got nine tenths already.!"

"Yep, haven't seen the like since 'fifty-two!"

They run back and forth to all the fields to see if it's soaking in and then back to the radio to hear if it will continue and for how long.

Of course the women are busy making coffee for the guys who stop in to discuss the rain, while trying to contain at least some of the mud in the back porch.

Farmers get all romantic when the rain hits. Not in the ordinary sense of the word. Still, it's romantic.

"Gee, Bets, look it's coming straight down!"

Well, as long as I can remember, rain has come "straight down" but I'm not about to prick his balloon of happiness.

The farmer is the greatest gambler on earth and when the dice are rolled and the chips are down, he knows, as does his family, their future depends wholly on Mother Nature and her gift of rain.

Painting the Kitchen

Every spring I get the urge to revamp, clean, switch things about or change my curtains.

The sun's rays are stronger and everything takes on a shabby, dusty look. This look was there all winter, just not strong enough to get me into action.

For the first few weeks I'm usually content to rearrange things – the silk plant to the coffee table, the brass elephant to the mantle – soon I realize this procrastination has to be dealt with and genuine scrubbing begins.

One spring I thought I might even do a bit of painting. Not the canvas and oil type of painting; no I mean the covering of chips and dents which had occurred over the year.

Bill has always been the self-appointed painter in the family. He feels, with good reason, I am too sloppy. Of course, when he painted, I still had to run ahead dusting, behind with coffee and on hand always for orders.

But this time I decided I'd try my own hand at this elusive art. So one spell when he had to be away for at least two days, I decided to paint the woodwork in the kitchen.

First I went to town for paint and brushes. I knew I didn't dare touch his. They are his pride and joy and are always cleaned out to perfection and hung with great care.

I had decided to change the color of the kitchen woodwork to make it more interesting. It was a soft yellow and I felt I'd like to use a brighter color to cheer the room.

As I flipped through the various shades available in the paint store, I spied one which not only looked pretty but had such a romantic name, "Sea Foam Green." I bought enough to paint the barn as I didn't want to be short, also a huge can of turpentine for clean-ups.

At home, I found a pile of newspapers which I spread hither and yon and stirred up the paint. A panic attack struck – what if I really couldn't paint? What if I botched it so badly it needed redoing?

"Nuts!" I said and started in.

The first thing I noticed was that this was no soft shade of sea foam. This was bright – really bright! Still, I figured it would soften as it dried.

I painted like fury all day, never stopping for more than a quick cup of tea. By seven I had finished the first coat but had run out of energy and a good bit of enthusiasm. The kitchen was a shambles. I didn't care. I ate a bowl of cornflakes and tumbled into the bed I hadn't made.

I woke up a 5 a.m. and ran out to the kitchen to view my handiwork. Well, it definitely hadn't dried a softer shade. Instead it literally glowed!

To see what it would look like with a second coat, I leaned over to paint a strip. My housecoat swept into the paint can and slopped down on my bare foot. Even this didn't dampen my newly resurrected zeal, so I climbed into my paint clothes and hit it once more.

The second coat was much easier to apply and by 4 p.m. I was all finished with the floor even washed. I was so pleased with myself – I had actually painted – and not too badly.

Beth and Mitch came in and Mitch burst out laughing.

"Does it glow in the dark?" he dared ask.

He didn't faze my pride of a job well done. I had completed what I set out to do with the only casualties being two green-bottomed socks and a newly decorated housecoat.

Of course, the newly painted woodwork made the wallpaper look shabby. So I decided I'd have to paper the kitchen.

Just try matching Sea Foam green. I found the lid of my oven cleaner was a perfect match so armed with that, my daughter Pat and I viewed every single roll of paper in central Alberta. No luck.

I was about to give up when I spotted one I thought perfect.

"Pat, look – I've found it!"

She looked at it and burst out laughing. "Mom, that's the one you've got on the walls now!"

Ordering Garden Seeds

I could resist the urge no longer – I ordered my garden seeds today.

The miracle was I managed to keep the cost below last year's order – but I remembered the fuss I caused at this time last year when I told Bill what they came to!

I've always found it hard to control myself when ordering plants and seeds. Back when I grew a vegetable garden, I'd find myself knee-deep in produce each and every year. One year it was string beans, five rows of them about a rod long produced too many beans even for our busy household. Even my Hutterite friends didn't plant that many – I had beans coming out my ears. I pickled, froze and canned enough beans to feed the crowds at the Second Coming. My friends would run and bolt the doors when I came over the hill with yet another basket brimming over.

Another disaster my kids won't let me forget – the time I ordered one pound of carrot seeds. We love carrots, so I thought I'd get extra. "My, I'll be able to freeze some for stews and think of the carrot cakes I can make!" I enthused.

Well, when the time came to planting them, I realized my mistake – one pound of carrot seed is a lot!

I planted and planted until I realized if I didn't stop, I'd have no room left to plant potatoes. I think I planted 17 rows of carrots until, in final desperation, I tossed the rest over the fence into the bull corral. It didn't seem to hurt them except their eyes took on a strange yellow hue for a few days.

Next to perfume and shoes, flower seeds and plants are my downfall. If the seed companies wouldn't make their illustrations so beautiful, I'd stand a chance but every picture is designed to turn you weak with envy. You can just see those flowers blooming in your garden. Even if it clearly states, "suitable only for Timbuktu" I talk myself into trying them.

"Oh, I can always cover them if need be and put out candles to ward off the frost!"

Another problem I have is remembering the names of the ones I had success with the year before. I've ordered lavatera instead of phlox. I've squished out my pansies, put lily of the valley to the east and begonias to the south. Still, every spring my mind blanks this out and my rosy vision snaps into gear.

Ordering lots of seeds and plants is fine and dandy if one's enthusiasm keeps up through the growing season. Usually by the time the seed order arrives from Bowden, a particle of my vigor has worn off. By the time the weeds are poking through, I'm growling about, snarling at everyone about how hard it is to get help in the garden.

However, as of today, I'm brimful of vigor and vitality so my order was a little lengthy. Bill did complain some, until I stopped him with a reminder.

"Fine, I'll just let this place go back to prairie sod and I'll sell the lawn mower!"

Whether it was my attempt at blackmail or whether he just wanted to shut me up, I don't know. He shook his head and handed me the money, so now I'll wait with baited breath for these harbingers of spring to arrive. Hmm, I wonder if I could grow another rose or two?

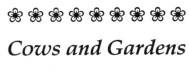

Cows and Gardens

❀ ❀ ❀ ❀ ❀ ❀ ❀ ❀ ❀

Cattle are wonderful and gardens delightful. The two together can be a deadly combination.

I have a steady, ongoing war with the cattle and haven't won the battle yet. I like gardening and for many years I planted a big enough vegetable garden to feed a Hutterite colony. I tried to plant it with care and took great pride in going out early in the morning to gaze at it. True, the rows were not too straight and the seed depth depended on how lumpy the ground was but it always provided enough food for our family for a hard winter. My flower garden is still a great joy to me. Oh, I'm not a fussy gardener but I love flowers and am always looking for another root from anyone within the radius of 500 miles.

This gardening takes a lot of work as any expert will tell you. Do the cows care? Not likely!

They have a built in radar system which starts buzzing the second the last seed is in the ground and the last plant carefully patted in. This radar leads them to the most vulnerable spot in the whole garden.

Now they are not content to merely meander around placidly – no, they must kick up their heels and buck about, bunting each other in great glee, so by the time they are finally rooted out and safely back in the pasture, the poor garden looks like the surface of the moon, craters and all.

The seeds have been transplanted so deeply the only things to survive are the onion sets and even those have to be lifted.

I can handle some of this with a certain amount of grace but when they cut through the bedding out plants I come out fighting.

Last year I planted seventy dollars' worth of plants and no blooming cow was going to wreck them. After all, I had spent four tough negotiating hours with Bill talking him into the worth of so much stuff we couldn't eat.

I break an average of two good broom handles a year on the backs of retreating cattle and I'm sure my yelling can be heard in town. Maybe that's why the cows seem to enjoy getting out so much. After all, the pasture or feed lot can be downright boring, at least until the bulls are turned out in June.

It seems there's always one cow in every herd who loves to lead the way. If the others fail to follow she wanders around my garden like a sick goose in a thunderstorm all by her lonesome.

One such cow just loved petunias. Every night she'd crawl through the fence and nip off the flowers, leaving great holes where she walked. Muttering away, I'd fill the holds and prop up the survivors.

Finally after the twentieth time or so, I threw a grand snit, an art I've perfected over the years. With much relief, I saw Bill and the hired man heading out with fencing pliers and staples.

It did rather unnerve me when I heard Bill mutter to Peter, "We'd better keep that poor cow away from Bets. She might just drop her calf with all that yelling in her ear!"

Bridal Shower Gifts

I went to a bridal shower the other night and took my usual gift. Now, 99 percent of the ladies give gifts of crystal, fine linen and elegant china. Me? I give tools.

It isn't because I'm cheap. No, it's because I know what a bride will need. It doesn't matter whether she is marrying a farmer, a rancher, a bank manager or a lawyer. No matter what her home will be, a castle or a sod shack, she'll need tools.

It took me awhile to realize I needed a set of tools of my very own. For years I used my rolling pin for a hammer. It worked well although my pie crusts were decorated with strange designs from all the dents the nailheads left in the wooden rolling pin. For a heavy job I used the heel of Bill's riding boot.

I used a kitchen knife for a screwdriver and a nail file for any filing jobs. For anything that needed gluing I used nail polish and for putty I used chewing gum.

Gradually I built up a real tool collection, buying one or two items at a time. At the beginning I made the mistake of buying good ones, so good the men would snitch them. From then on I bought real cheap ones, three-dollar hammers and Bill wouldn't lower himself to use anything so inferior. I also raided the shop when the coast was clear and took back what I thought they owed me until finally I had a nice little tool set all my own.

I keep it in a plastic bag in my junk drawer and no one in their right mind ever tries to find anything in that drawer.

I've noticed over the years I've become quite daring. At first when I was new to the bridal lifestyle I would wait for Bill to hang a picture, fix a chair rung or replace a screw. As you know, farmers are so busy solving great worldly problems – the GST, the Wheat Board or what to do about the plight of the farmer – that there just wasn't time for such things as a collapsing chair. So I started doing these small jobs by myself.

A nail here, a screw there and a dab of paint wherever needed. It wasn't long before I realized I was enjoying this challenge. Of course I made lots of errors. There are dents in the walls to prove it but I am improving all the time. I now can tap a nail in as straight as an arrow and I've had only one black thumb nail this year. I've hung pictures so well my kids stare at them in awe – although this might be because I use the odd staple when I can't find a nail.

My greatest achievement thus far is my trellises. Our house is old, built in 1914. The house has helped raise two generations of rambunctious kids with a third one now running. The verandah gave way so Bill poured cement and built a deck about four feet off the ground. This left a blank space of ugliness which bothered me. So one day when he was out west gathering cattle and I knew he wouldn't be home for a couple of days, I decided to rectify this eyesore.

I measured the length and width and tore into town for some trellising. On getting it home I found to my dismay it stuck up too high. So I went to the shop and found a handsaw marked "RIP," the significance of which I couldn't figure out. Anyway, it sawed fine. I had to lay the trellis across the picnic table and prop one foot on it to hold it steady.

After the sawing was done I nailed the sections on and painted them. My I was pleased with myself. For the next three days I'd run out every once in awhile to gaze upon my handiwork. After the second coat of paint it was a sight to behold.

So you see why I like to give tools as shower gifts. Just maybe one of those brides will turn out to be a sculptor with a hammer.

Oh yes, I did learn that "RIP" on a saw does not mean rest in peace – it's a special saw for sawing lengthwise! Any other questions, just phone the expert!

Spring Cleaning

A lot of young women today have never heard of "Spring Cleaning." They are the homemakers who are wise enough and sufficiently organized to keep their homes spanking clean at all times.

Then, there's the rest of us, of various ages, who were raised with Spring Cleaning. Actually, the habit started years ago when the west was settled and the pioneer women went through this ritual every spring.

Part of the reason, I'm sure, was the fact the women didn't have the time to clean thoroughly every week. Housekeeping was harder back then with few of the conveniences we have today. The homes were rougher and much harder to keep up. Besides, the pioneer woman was usually so busy milking cows, gardening, scrubbing clothes by hand and canning hundreds of quarts of every fruit and vegetable available, there was precious little time for extra cleaning. She had to settle for a general run-through on Saturdays. When spring arrived, she cut loose with great fervor and energy gave everything a thorough cleaning.

Every window was stripped and washed inside and out, the curtains washed and starched, rugs hauled out and the very dickens beaten out of them, mattresses, if store-bought, aired outside and if filled with straw, emptied and refilled with fresh stuffing.

The whole house was scrubbed with an ammonia mixture so strong everyone's noses ran for a good week. Even the stove pipes were taken down and gingerly hauled outside for their annual cleaning.

New fly coils replaced the old ones which, by spring, were hanging limp and heavy with dead bodies.

The outside biffy was scoured with a lye mixture so strong you were afraid to sit down for a good month. A sack of chloride of lime was tossed down the hole for good measure. This was the time the old catalogue was brought out to use for paper and any sayings written by some clandestine hand, scrubbed off the walls.

Oh, it was certainly a time of frenzy, that week of Spring Cleaning. There's still quite a few who carry on the tradition. I, for one, do. It's a sort of virus I seem to catch every April.

All winter long I'm quite calm and placid, getting an urge to clean only if company is coming and then doing only the necessities. By March a bull could bed down in the house and I'd hardly notice but when April arrives, I find myself cleaning out nail holes with a toothpick and starching the wallpaper. The sun's rays are strong, showing every little smear and I turn into some sort of a whirling dervish with a wet cloth. Of course by the time I'm on the last room, I find myself wiping plates with the floor rag and kicking a salami heel down the heat register!

Inevitably, when I'm in the throes of cleaning I get company -not the ordinary drop-in sort, I mean the type who are just acquaintances, new in town and who have never seen the messy side of me.

Having to climb over, around and under dangerous objects of all sizes does little to relax them. All they get is coffee because I never bake when house cleaning. I'm not exactly a glamor queen either, with my hair sticking every which way, dressed in chore jeans and wearing shoes only if I'm able to find them.

One thing I've learned through the years, your garbage barrel is your best friend during such times. In it you can dispose of a wealth of mistakes; the jeans you let the bleach slop on; your sewing errors, like the dress with the delightful measurements (60-20-30); the curtains your mother-in-law gave you which she felt had at least another forty years of wear in them.

You do have to be quick, though or you'll find all the stuff being hauled back in with statements like, "Mom, that's my very best mouse skin, how could you be so cruel!" Or "Gosh, Bets, I wore that cap when I was in Glasgow" (during the Second World War!)

So I always find it a good idea to toss a bit of diesel fuel on things before setting them ablaze. Bill caught me once after I had started a fire. It was really snorting with gusts of black smoke billowing higher than the TV antenna.

"Bets, what did you do?"

"Oh, I put a bit of diesel on it 'cause it was peelings!"

"Gosh, how much did you use, a quart?"

A quart? I had tossed a half a chop pail on it but I wasn't telling!

Meals always take on rather strange shapes and odours, for how can a woman cook when she's spring cleaning? It works well too – the fridge gets emptied of all sorts of bits and desserts are unheard of but boy the house is beginning to sparkle!

The whole family is so relieved when you have finally recovered from the virus – meals are normal, the house can be toured without breaking a leg and Mom is back to her old self.

I firmly believe the biggest thrill of housecleaning is not the shining domain you end up with, it's the fact you've finally got everything back to normal and you don't have to go through it again for another 11 months!

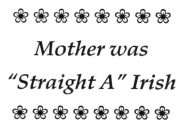

Mother was "Straight A" Irish

Saint Patrick's Day always sends my thoughts winging back to my childhood, with good reason. My own mother was "Straight A" Irish, born and raised in Tipperary.

Anyone thinking the fuss in Ireland is something new, best think again. They were fighting for their rights in 1919 – that's how Dad met Mother!

He was a Scot, a Highlander. After fighting in the First World War, he joined the Irish constabulary and was sent over to Ireland to help tame the rebellious Irish. Quite a challenge in itself, for the Irish have fought and died for their beliefs for centuries. Dad had quite a task ahead of him.

I gather Dad did not spend all his time "taming" the Irish race, for he met, courted and married Mother and all on his leave time.

They came out to Canada to a Soldier Settlement homestead. My brother, sister and I were the end result. I was often given to understand I was still fighting the Irish battles, right here in Canada.

As a child I'd do anything to get Mom to relate some of her "Irish stories," the tales of her childhood. I'd fold wash, iron, even do the dishes willingly, a feat in itself, to be able to hear those tales once more. When told with an Irish brogue, somehow the stories were even more romantic.

Mom's father and his father before him were farmers and raised beautiful race horses which they sold to the landed gentry of the time. As Mom told these stories I could feel myself riding a huge, beautiful black stallion, the wind blowing through my hair as I flew over bogs and fences.

Mom could talk, too. I've come to believe all Irish people have the gift of the silver tongue, so even a tale about eating a potato or a cabbage was turned into an exciting romance of taste, flavor and texture, filled with warmth and nostalgia.

At night I'd lie in my bed and make-believe I was on my grandparent's farm back in Ireland, quite a task for a kid who had never even been to Calgary. I'd be sitting in front of a huge stone fireplace, two hounds beside me, listening for the fairies' whisper in my ear.

I'd walk the stone walls, feeling the granite beneath my feet. I'd skip over the green grass and smell the smoke from the peat burning.

Besides being raised with Irish tales, I was also raised with thoughts of fairies and leprechauns. For years, I kept my own leprechaun, called Jezebel, in an old Roger's Golden Syrup can. A rather odd name for such a fairy, it was inspired by a biblical girl with such a name I'd heard of from the Anglican minister. I thought it a delightful name.

I was also raised with the Irish language although I didn't realize it was any different from the norm until I was in grade five. I could see nothing strange about being sent out for "kipeens" to hurry the fire along but when I sent some flunkies for kipeens at CGIT camp, they came back with minnows in a bucket of slough water. They thought I meant kippers and the nearest things to kippers in Fish Lake were minnows.

Shoes gave me a bit of trouble. Every other kid in the class had "penny loafers." I had the self-same ones, only mine were called "brogues." I couldn't see that mine were exactly like the rest. Mother called them "brogues," so they must be different and for a young girl to be different is equivalent to being banished from the earth.

I also knew the Irish term for "boiler." Three times a week I was sent to the creamery with two pails to fill the "biler." I think I was about ten when I found out I wasn't speaking Western Canadian. I had approached the creamery manager to ask if I could get enough water to fill the "biler" and he, being a German, muttered, "Why can't you speak right? There's no such thing as a 'biler.' Bile, yes, in your belly, biler, no!"

I told mother one day that I thought she should start calling it a boiler or a tub. That's what old Swertz said.

Mother snorted. "How would a German know? They can only grunt and eat garlic!"

The odd Gaelic phrase often popped up with disastrous results. On one such occasion Mom was telling Dad about the banker's wife getting a new set of teeth from the dentist who came out from Calgary once a month. I couldn't remember her wording exactly but despite her accent and odd words I had figured it all out. The banker's wife was running around with the dentist and was leaving her husband next month. I was feeling quite important as I passed this news on to all and sundry. Oh my, was there a hubbub.

When it was all straightened out and it was learned I was the culprit, I was in the dog house for a good month. After times like these I'd hear Mother speaking to the neighbor over the back fence.

"Ooch doosen. What else can you expect with her Father's Scottish blood running through her veins!"

Summertime in the Country

Bill, I Trimmed the Tree
(and it's not even Christmas!)

It's just about time to clean up the lawn mowers and stick them away for the winter. Where did the summer go?

Lawn mowers and I have had a shaky partnership ever since I first started using them and many a cup of tea I've had to sip to calm my nerves after one of these encounters.

Of course three quarters of the time it's my own fault, not the mower's. Knowing this only adds to the drama.

On most farms there is little planted lawn, all flat and even, a joy to cut. Most of the grass is prairie sod which down through the years has held everything from brooder houses to barns, had horses harnessed on top of it, machines fixed and even the odd ash pile dumped there.

This history adds great drama to the simple act of cutting the grass because remnants of its past keep surfacing and clogging up even the most basic lawn mower. Bits of wire, rocks, old spikes and the awful plastic baler twine play havoc with the machine as well as with the operator.

Add this to the fact that I'm not mechanically minded and you have an interesting combination.

For me, when I have the time to trim the place up a bit, I want to do nothing more than crawl on the mower and turn the key, without having to think of all the intricacies of machinery. I want to ride around and think lovely thoughts! This never seems possible. I run over plastic twine, which, instead of cutting, wraps itself around the blades so tightly it chokes the life out of the thing. The only way to dislodge the twine is to tip the machine over and cut it off strand by strand. But when I attempt this, the oil runs into something or other and the machine won't start again. So I have to hunt all over the farm for a likely looking male figure to come and get it started.

One thing I learned the hard way was to keep topping up the oil. One seized motor taught me that.

When my riding mower, which is small and basic in design, is on the hummer – once a year at least – I resort to my little push mower. This one is old and decrepit.This summer when I dragged it out I noticed the gas tank was hanging loose, there were splits here and there and when I started it the vibrations which shot up the handle just about shook my arms off. I wanted to finish a piece of grass I had about half done, so I stuck a big spike in the hole where a screw had fallen out. Then I checked the oil. Over-zealously, I filled it to the brim – killing it with kindness, I soon found out. I pulled the starter rope and *WHEW* – Chernobyl again. A cloud of black smoke rose on the wind and wafted off through the bushes before the motor quit.

I tried and tried. With each yank of the starter rope the engine emitted a great dense black cloud. I gave up and at suppertime hit Bill with my problem. He took a look at the oil and patiently, as though he were instructing a moron, gave me a lesson on the proper reading of dip sticks.

"Now Betsy, see this line. It's there for a reason. It says full. Can you see it? Well, you put three times too much oil in it!" He gave the machine a shake and realized it was in need of something he didn't want to give it – an overhaul.

"Take this over to Air Cool John's and he'll fix it for you." He walked off leaving me with the urge to kick him in the rear.

Air Cool John is a long-suffering friend who lives in Torrington and fixes small engines, etc. He's laid back and good at this work. He has fixed my minor disasters for years and had my riding mower at the time, waiting for parts. As I drove in with my wreck, John came out, gave a great sigh and stated, "Betty, I think you should buy a goat."

When I finally got both machines back and was feeling that just maybe I'd get through all the grass before something else broke, I inadvertently pushed "forward" instead of "reverse" and climbed a tree. I found myself flat on my back with my legs still in position on the lawn mower, which was trying valiantly to climb to the upper branches. After I turned off the mower and quit hyperventilating, I crawled off and pulled the thing down. The poor tree still hasn't recovered as all the bark was scraped off its trunk.

Two weeks later, as I was rounding a corner both hind wheels, axle and all, fell off with a thud. Now a lesser person might have had a nervous breakdown. I only yelled and whined until Bill got a nice new one.

While thinking about my troubles with lawn mowers, I remembered the first one I had, an old cylinder with a with blade inside. No motor, just me pushing. The only gas you ran out of was your own but it played havoc with your energy level.

So I really should be thankful.

Gold in Fly Spots

Guess what I read yesterday? "Fly Spots" are worth their weight in gold! I could hardly believe my eyes but that's what the article said. Just think of all the wealth we've lost via the scrub rag and brush over the years. It makes one shudder in pain. Even so, my house is worth a fortune as it stands today.

This isn't all guff, either. It seems that any item in an antique shop which boasts a few fly spots is worth far more than those without. Such speckles seem to have replaced the lofty wormholes in furniture and you know how important they grew to be.

But the article stated you're not "in" unless you own at least two or three antique pieces adorned with fly spots. Paintings, old calenders, posters, even vases are "worth their weight in gold" if they are decorated with lots of spots!

I imagine they are protected by a good coat of varnish and kept safely away in a china cupboard or drawer just waiting for a likely buyer or else willed to some unsuspecting kin. It would be a crime if our children and grandchildren grew up without ever seeing a fly spot!

The awful part of it is the day before I read this mind-boggling news, I had waged the mother of all wars on the priceless winged creatures. With the help of Bills's spray can and enough spray to cover Belgium, I hit the farm. Corrals, feed lots, watering holes, the barnyard, everywhere the things hang out. The smell was a bit much and I was awfully thankful I had plastic gloves on as I really dosed them. The garbage barrels, the loading chute and even the verandah got the works.

By the time I was finished I smelled like DDT and ached in every bone of my body. It was worth it.

I came in, stripped and after a hot bath, sat back with a cup of tea, feeling very smug at my usefulness around the place.

Then I happened to pick up that blasted magazine. Here I had held a fortune in my hands and blew it. I could have been the first person in the district to hone in on this lucrative market.

Just think, I could have put out some vases and other junk I've been saving for a garage sale, let the flies do their thing, then sold them to antique stores all over Alberta. Mine would be real authentic fly spots – not some cheap imitation. I was absolutely mortified at this lost opportunity.

I can't help but wonder what our forefathers would think – they had fought the good fight with fly coils and swatters all those years and now this. It was almost sacrilegious!

I have a funny feeling they might think as I do – money isn't everything and beauty is in the eye of the beholder.

Besides, as I look about I still have a few spots I can save for posterity and now I'll get out of washing around my lights. We don't want to do away with part of our history, do we?

Summer-Fallowing

I think the thing I hate the most of all about farming as an occupation is summer-fallowing. Land work, rod weeding, whatever you wish to call it. Don't get me wrong. I love this rural way of life and wouldn't want any other but when the men are working the land it's a blooming nuisance.

Just when you breathe a great sigh of relief because you've been informed that the last kernel of grain is safely planted and you hope a shopping day in the city might possibly be in your future, you're greeted with a growl. "Now Bets, you should know, we've acres of summer fallow to do!"

I don't give up easily. "Lets just take off for a few hours. The weeds will wait!"

"Take off? This is the busy season, don't you know?"

As a farmer's wife of many years, I know the busy season on the farm is from January to December, every year.

Land work is so important! If you miss a single second, you're going to be out like Mulroney next election! The very thought of a wild oat peeping through the ground is a blight on the farmer's good name and will cause the downfall of the West. A field left undone for more than a few days is the shame of the land. A farmer can have an old tractor, a hole in the corral, a poor cook for a wife but poor summer fallow? NEVER!!

It isn't just the time it takes to keep up the fallowed land or the importance placed on it that's so irritating. It's the unholy mess the house becomes when they are doing it.

The men come in so black you'd think they were tilling with their heads and when they wash up, to use the term loosely, they splash water all over their faces with great gusto and noise and on down their arms to slosh on the floor in great black puddles.

Little Miss Perfect Housekeeper must either have a fainting spell or try to beat the men to death at such times. The rest of us just wipe it up and sigh, counting the days until the land work is finished and the men are into haying.

What this wash-up really reminds me of is an elephant in Africa splashing in a mud hole.

I'm not really sure why they bother using water at all. Maybe it's just to loosen the dirt so it will wipe off well on the towel! You can put a clean towel out and in four minutes it resembles something used for calving last winter after which the dog dragged it around.

But "to feel clean is to be clean," says an old proverb. And so they are content to plop down on the chairs with a sigh, which raises a great cloud of dust from their bottoms.

Needless to say, they leave a trail from door to table to bath and even to bed – ample proof of what work they are busy at. Even the sheets and pillowcases are black enough to raise a three-bushel crop on their own. The men's teeth, hair, clothes, even their eyes are black and there's usually enough dirt in their ears to plant potatoes.

But it does end. I try once more. "Well, now that you've finished the summer fallow, let's take off!"

"Goodness, Bets, maybe first rain we can but that first field I did is showing thistles. I gotta start it in the morning!"

Thistles

❀ ❀ ❀ ❀

Thistles – the bane of my life.

Since the day I took up gardening, they have been trying with great success to irritate, aggravate and finish me off.

One would wonder why a simple little thistle could cause so much grief. They are much the same as any weed, made up of leaves, stems and a dash of chlorophyll.

Don't kid yourself, they are as deadly as a delayed time bomb and pack enough punch to turn a warrior into a gibbering idiot.

My little flower garden is a basic one . . . a few roses, columbines, asters and such. In amongst the perennials, I plant petunias, snapdragons, and some zinnias. The soil is average and the moisture adequate.

What's so terrible, you ask? Well, every two inches throughout the whole garden spot is that ordinary little plant – a few leaves, a stem and a dash of chlorophyll – the thistle. Trouble is, it's got a root which must be fourteen feet long!

Dig them out, you say? Good heavens, I've been digging them out for years, each and every summer. I've dug more than it took to dig the Panama canal. I can't tell you how many spades and forks I've worn out, not to mention sneakers. I dig and dig and dig. I've been told I have to get the whole root. Well when you dig a hole big enough to bury a bull, you should, by all reasonable chances, get the whole root!

In fact, I've supposedly got the whole root so many times I've given up counting. That long grey creature usually runs under every plant I've got, the sidewalk and the old back porch.

I'm sure thistles have this foreign type of breeding program. When you dig up the big Daddy one and toss it away, the Mother gets all uptight and pops seven or eight little ones to keep the breed going. These she dutifully instructs, in ways known only to thistles, how to propagate the species and drive all humans stark raving mad, especially the one with the garden fork trying so valiantly to wipe them off the face of the earth.

I've tried so many different methods of dealing with thistles, I've lost count.

I was told to paint each plant with diesel fuel, so I filled an ice cream bucket with fuel, got my old paint brush and went to work. It took me a good morning and although it seemed I had painted the Sistine Chapel with a toothbrush by the time it was done, I just knew I got the little suckers! I ran out each morning for over a week to see them in their death throes. All they did was grow a little taller and add a leaf or two to their already healthy bodies.

Someone said to throw soapy water on them. It would take a barge-full to give them all a shot. I tried it anyway, with little effect.

Now, I fill an old syringe with Round-up and inject it into the main stalk each day for about a week. With this treatment they are slowly dying and along with lots of digging, I've got them at least under control.

What bothers me the most is when I find one in the centre of one of the perennials I've been pampering. I can almost hear the thing chuckling in malicious glee as I try to extricate it without disturbing the roots of my poor plant.

All I seem to manage is to split the thistle root so four more pop through the ground.

I wish so many times the blasted thistles were still back in Scotland and would leave me alone but then our Immigration officers would probably give them landed immigrant status or something.

I'm still digging away like a badger each summer day, so if you come to visit look in the garden first – the maniac digging away will be me!

❀❀❀❀❀❀❀❀❀❀❀

Fall on the Farm

❀❀❀❀❀❀❀❀❀❀❀

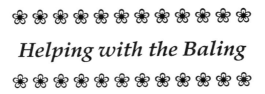

Helping with the Baling

There are times, as women know, when they are the only ones available to help in the fields as the weather threatens and something needs to be finished.

Baling can be one of the things the men need your assistance with. Even though I'm green when it comes to running machinery properly I can still pass on a few tips I've learned the hard way when drafted to help bale.

Once you've hoisted yourself up on the tractor, you are away – sometimes in more ways that one!

"Okay, Bets, this is the clutch. Let it out. Good. Now push it forward" This I do with such emphasis that I lift the front wheels off the ground a foot.

"No, no honey, not so hard!"

I'm not too disturbed because I'm still in the "honey" bracket. That was at the beginning. Finally, in desperation Bill puts in everything that needs to be in and starts me down the swath. I might mention here that anytime I helped him out he'd drag out the oldest tractor he owned in case I wrecked the good stuff – this was a distinct possibility!

Now the next thing I found out was that the baler follows the tractor so if you happen to turn too far right you cross not only one or two extra swathes, but also your husband's mind and he's not thinking up sweet nothings to whisper to you later!

Next, aim your front wheel beside the swath. You can see the front wheel but the only way to keep track of the back wheel is to lean way over – and this can affect your superb steering.

After mastering your steering you must move on to other little details. This will be those d____ corners! Maybe you can steer a car, turn a pick-up on a dime and handle a grocery cart but try it with a tractor and baler and you might find yourself in the bull pasture heading for the Herd Sire himself.

Of course the only thing you can do when the tractor takes off on a flight of fancy is steer it back and get into position once more. You'd best check behind you in case you've dumped your baling partner in your merry caper across the field!

The secret of the corners is to swing out a bit then turn back quickly so you can straighten up on the swath. If you do not turn quickly you'll find you've left 12 feet of swath untouched. Remember, 12 feet of swath can feed three cows for a whole day! You'll get adept at this manoeuvre if you keep a picture of a skinny cow pasted up in the tractor.

Once you've mastered the corners and can drive straight and let out the clutch with ease, you're a grade A baler. There are all sorts of other small things to learn but being as how this is a temporary position, you can bluff your way through.

The only thing left to learn is the art of spitting. That's right. It's the only way to clear all your tubes of all the dust and straw and can be quite impressive if you give a good snort in front of someone.

So don't worry, it's a great adventure. Where else can a lady spit and not cause raised eyebrows?

Silage and Me

Cattle are a wonderful investment. That's what any rancher will tell you. These same cattle, good investment though they be, have to be fed, and this on many ranches, entails silage making.

Silage time is exciting. It's such a relief to see that huge empty pit filling up with succulent greens for the long months of winter feeding ahead. It's a satisfying time for the men and it's a literal ball for all the kids in the district.

The women? They are so busy they haven't time to stop and enjoy the moment being so busy baking pies, peeling vegetables, taking out lunches and washing dishes by the dozen.

It always seems odd to me it takes 10 or 12 able-bodied men with an assortment of expensive machinery to fill one empty silage pit, whereas it takes only one woman with two hands to fill those 12 stomachs umpteen times a day! It speaks well for the women, I maintain.

I rather enjoy silage time. It brings out the pioneer instinct in me. I hold great admiration for our pioneer women who fed the old-time harvest crews of 20 to 25 men, all without the help of our modern appliances. No deep freezes for them. No cake mixes, store bought vegetables in fancy jars or even pie fillings. They made their own bread and butter, cooked on an old coal stove and even found time to boss the crew if the need arose.

One thing I've learned through practice is that you cannot do one other thing while silage time is on. Hide the ironing in the closet and don't look at the kitchen floor – even if you stick to it. By the time you're through one meal and get the dishes washed it's time to start the next. I always had the dubious honor of trotting out with lunches in-between the regular meals. I remember when I first started all this foolishness, Bill coached me.

"Bets, do wear that little red gingham dress and make that chocolate cake I like!"

"Honey, now don't forget a little lipstick!"

"So and so only brought coffee, so don't forget the sandwiches!"

I got the feeling I was being set up, rather like an Egyptian slave girl up for market with little in her favor. I soon put a stop to this nonsense.

The men arrive for meals on time and always in a good frame of mind. They never complain about the food but then I'm fairly convinced I could set out bowls of chop for them and they'd eat it without noticing. Men are gossips, especially when they get together, and each meal, items of great importance are hashed over, the price of cattle, the drop in wheat sales and the 16 heifers they plan to buy.

Our kids always had a wonderful time jumping into the silage pit. The landing is soft and juicy and boy could they leap. The odd shoe got left in the pit until I gave orders: bare feet only. They could turn summersaults, flips and do all sorts of other leaps. Getting the silage color out of the clothes was a bit of a challenge. Bleach helped. Skin was a real problem. Each year I'd fervently pray the sickly yellow color would wear off before school started. I had visions of the teacher panicking – the child has jaundice! Send him home!

What a good feeling when the silage pit is filled and there's lots of feed for another year.

Halloween

❀ ❀ ❀ ❀ ❀

There's something unique about Halloween. It warms people's hearts.

I always enjoyed Halloween, although we live in the country and get only a few neighborhood kids and our own little ones. Each year I find myself buying enough treats for half the town and finding just the right pumpkin to carve a scary face into.

Halloweens have changed. Mothers are hesitant to let their little ones out by themselves. Fast traffic and adults hanging about and big kids who swipe bags make them worry. Each bag brought home has to be thoroughly searched for razor blades and poison. It's sad. Now small communities are putting on great parties in halls, so all kids will be safe and still enjoy the excitement of the night.

When I was a kid there was little that could happen to injure us, so both parents and kids relaxed and enjoyed the night.

We pulled a few tricks we thought daring, giggled and screamed a lot and hit every house in town, sometimes twice if we could get away with it. We'd pass the word along if one place gave out extra special treats – rather like the hobos of the thirties who marked the gate of the generous, so others on the road knew it was a good place to approach.

One year I remember well. It was during wartime when candy was extremely scarce. The mothers all made cookies and improvised popcorn balls and that was about it.

All us kids, while discussing our plan of attack, decided to include the restaurant. For some reason we had never approached this establishment other years.

We were in luck. The lady handed out chocolate bars – one big one for each kid! Boy, were we thrilled. We could hardly wait to get home and show off our treasures. Most of us hardly ever saw candy. To actually have a whole chocolate bar was totally awesome!

But when we finally tore off the wrapper we found, to our total horror, they were wormy! And I mean wormy – not just one or two little skinny worms, I mean totally!! No wonder the lady handed them out with so much goodwill.

Now a kid's horror is much more dramatic and noisy than an adult's, so you can just imagine the scene repeated through the town that night as the story was told and retold.

We counted each worm, dissected them, watched them wiggle and then saved them to show everyone the next day at school.

I believe about forty wormy chocolate bars showed up and were squealed over. Actually, it was much more exciting to get a wormy bar than a good apple or a popcorn ball.

The years sped by and soon we felt we were much too mature for going trick-or-treating like little children. We spent one year staying home handing out treats with bored looks on our faces but by the next year we had decided to advance further to the really mature hobby of playing stupid tricks!

That is a year I'll never forget. Six of us girls, all supposedly nice girls of about fifteen years of age, planned on the ultimate adventure. We would tip over a toilet! We cased the back alley for just the right one. It was huge, a double seater and quite sturdy looking. We walked up and around it, deciding at which angle it would go over easiest. I'm sure if anyone had noticed six girls, all quiet and respectable, spending so much time in discussion in an alley, they would have figured we were out on a school project. After all, we were in CGIT and sang in the church choir.

When the night finally arrived, we met and about ten o'clock quietly crept up the alley. We each took our position around the toilet and gave a mighty heave. Over it went with a crash. Before it hit the ground, we heard the most God-awful screech which sounded like an Irish banshee. The blasted toilet was occupied!

We nearly died we were so petrified. When we saw a pair of long skinny white legs coming after us, we were gone. By the time the poor woman had crawled free, we were at the corner but she was right after us. We ran and ran, our sides aching and our breaths coming in mournful gasps. Finally, we reached the park at the far end of the town and collapsed in the deep grass. We stayed there until well after midnight, so had ample time to worry before we crept home, cold and miserable.

Guilt is quite an amazing thing. The next day we waited for the town policeman to show up and haul us off to reform school at the very least. Neither the lady nor the police showed up and to this day not a soul but us knows the true tale of that trick.

That was the year we really grew up. The outhouse went up the next day and is still standing in all its glory.

4H Daze

❀ ❀ ❀ ❀

I've always been a strong defender of 4H clubs and what they stand for. I'm always for anything that will keep the kids off the street and busy; anything good that doesn't let boredom set in!

Our own kids were in the Beef Club and Bill is a former leader. So every chance we get, we like to support 4H.

I truly believe a child lucky enough to be a member of 4H gets a head start on adult life. They learn responsibility and it gives them a good grounding in keeping records. Their Public Speaking training is wonderful, although I'm sure at times it must scare them spitless to get up and speak in front of a group. And raising and fitting a calf for the show and the sale is an awesome responsibility.

Actually, the fun begins in November when the great bartering takes place. After walking through the herd seventeen times, the only calf the young 4Her wants is a purebred Hereford which Dad has destined for greater things! When it is knocked out of the competition, the real fuss begins.

There's something wrong with every other one. Too long, too short, too thick, too weak in the withers. Finally, after three hours, she chooses the first one they looked at.

The fuss isn't over. Now the cost squeeze begins. With market reports from the last two years laid out on the kitchen table, the talk begins.

This starts off quite sensibly and quietly and Dad thinks, "Gee, maybe it's going to be easier this year!" No way.

"Dad, that's too much – I won't make a cent! Really Dad, I don't see why you have to charge me for the feed."

"I can't raise it for less and that's final!"

"Cheapskate!"

A price is finally decided on, after much groaning and muttering and ten cups of strong coffee for Dad.

The winter months are peaceful except for the odd bit of coaxing trying to keep her working on her calf.

But oh, the halter breaking! And then the leading! Both calf and girl face each other with fear and hope intermingled. Neither calf nor girl is too sure of themselves. The initial round is terrible, with the calf getting away six times and the girl heading to the house in tears an equal number of times.

As time goes on, the odd fence gets laid low as a wildly running calf and a screaming, long-legged teenager go whistling by. With lots of guts and stamina, she gradually gets it under control.

Another worry arises. She suddenly figures the calf hasn't gained enough weight.

"I can't take that skinny thing to the show!" She snorts. "They would probably disqualify it!"

Soon she's so busy brushing, washing and leading the calf each spare moment, she's too tired to worry about its weight. They have learned to respect each other and love sets in.

All Mom's Fleecy is used up and the calf is as calm as a cucumber. Pride takes the place of disappointment and love takes the place of fear.

Mother is dragging a bit, though. During the past two weeks she has patched up wire cuts and built up courage in both calf and daughter. Now she realizes in just a few short hours her work on this project will be over.

By achievement day the calf is behaving beautifully and is shining like a new penny. He's tolerated the noisy clippers and his face is shiny clean and looking elegant in his new haircut. His proud mistress is equally as polished, from boots to hat, with the 4H emblem sewn on her shirt.

Soon the two take their place in the ring, all ready for the judge to look them over. She wins second in Showmanship and third for the calf. Not too bad. Then sadness creeps in. The calf which she loves is about to be sold to someone to eat! She uses a Kleenex or two when the calf's sold but she's got a bit of money for her holidays.

As they drive home, she turns to her dad and says, "How does the calf crop look, Dad? Is there a good one for me for next year?

Me and My Shotgun

I knew when I married Bill I was becoming part of a great hunting family. Bill's father had been a gamekeeper in Scotland and this love of the land and hunting stayed with him all his life. He was a guide and outfitter, taking parties out west fishing and hunting for many years. Both Bill and his brother Glen followed in his footsteps. They were all crack shots with both shotgun and rifle and rarely came home without game.

I know the rage today is to ban all guns and hunting and let the animals rule the world. But these men were probably the first of the conservationists, never taking more than their quota, knowing each animal and their track and taking special care of their horses before themselves. They have a natural love for all wild creatures and are naturalists more than many desk-thumping moralists who wouldn't know a pigeon from a pack rat.

At first, I would only shoot the .22 but Bill wanted me to learn the fine art of the shotgun. Now I didn't mind listening to the hunting stories and going to various shoots. But to actually shoot a shotgun – no thanks.

One day in a weak moment, I heard myself saying, "Okay!" to the worst proposition I've ever received: "Come on, honey, give it a try!"

Before I could collect my wits I was hauled out the front door and handed a .12-gauge single-barrel shotgun all loaded and ready to go.

"Okay Bets, pull it tight to your shoulder and squeeze gently!"

I pulled the trigger and thought I had set off a land mine. That gun kicked so hard it flew out of my hands and sent me reeling over Bill and into the white rose bush.

Then, amid the gunsmoke and my ringing ears, I heard my husband console me with, "Bets, you'll have to learn how to stand at ready." I didn't ask him, "At ready for what?"

After three more tries I was so weak I could hardly walk in the door. Upon patching my scratches and taking an aspirin, I realized it had been fun. I was hooked.

Bill, a bit afraid he might harm his cook, went and bought me a neat little .16-gauge double-barrel Spanish shotgun. An old English veterinarian in town, a shotgun expert, shortened the stock and stuck a pad on it for me. I was ready for live action.

First chance, we took off after the elusive Canada Goose. I put on my red hat and jacket and a dash of "come hither" cologne and hit for the pits.

Over they came. The sky was a blanket of feathers. You couldn't see even a speck of blue sky as they winged their way just over our heads.

I leapt to my feet, closed my eyes and shot both barrels off, all in a second. I didn't get as much as a feather! How could I have missed? I loaded and reloaded, missing each and every time. Eyes open, eyes closed, one open – still not even a honk!

I finished off a whole carton of shells and had nothing to show for it but a sore shoulder and a red eye. Still, I practised every chance I got, squeezing the trigger, following with the barrel, everything I could think of.

Finally, one evening Bill and I were duck shooting at a slough and a lone duck came over. Not bothering about aiming, squeezing or leading, I up and took a wild shot, not thinking I could hit it anyway. But surprise, surprise, the fool duck fell! I had my first duck! I let out some war hoops so loud the flock that was coming in abruptly veered away but oh boy, I had my duck!

Actually, that was the only one I ever shot. Shortly after I retired my shotgun forever. How could I ever better such excellence?

❁ ❁ ❁ ❁ ❁ ❁ ❁ ❁

Winter Sports

❁ ❁ ❁ ❁ ❁ ❁ ❁ ❁

The Common Cold

Is there anything really common about the "common cold?" I doubt it.

Look at the shelves and shelves of medicine across the land, medicines promising to alleviate the symptoms, let you sleep, keep you awake and relieve your pain. All types of cold medicine with prices that cure your cold just looking at them.

Along with these go the vitamins and minerals which are supposed to build up your immunity to this "common bug." Pink ones, yellow ones, tasty ones, bitter ones and ones for kids in cartoon figures. I've never been able to figure out why it's easier for a kid to swallow Fred Flintstone than a cheap white one. I guess that's just due to my age.

I had to choose vitamins and cold medicines very carefully for our children when they were little. I soon learned if your kids turn against them, you're in trouble and your desire to improve your child's health can turn into an urgent need to throttle them.

The fuss is unbelievable and has left many a mother a quivering mass of jelly by the time the kids are on the school bus.

"I know you'll love these – they taste like bubble gum!"

"No, No, No," as the kid jumps around dodging the pills as though they were lit dynamite.

"Don't you want to be big like Daddy?"

"He never takes them!"

Dads and Moms did take them and their parents didn't have to coax, either. You see, back then, kids ate everything – it was part of the depression. They even split peach pits open to eat the nutty centres.

As for vitamins and cold pills, mothers used to threaten, the opposite way. "Straighten up or no pills for you tonight!" and everyone turned into little angels. Instead of "Please, honey, it tastes good!" she'd toss them out like a peanut scramble and turn the kids loose. So what if they got three vitamin C and one iron? It all evened out by spring.

Mothers used to line the kids up and Dad would march along dishing a spoon of cod liver oil into each open mouth. It was as close to a treat as the kids would get until Christmas and during the war years they didn't want to miss it.

Thinking back, this treatment seemed to work. It was administered from October to May and I can't recall any epidemics or kids missing school due to colds. Of course, missing school might have been the worse alternative. If you got a really severe chest cold, you were wrapped in blankets, laid in bed and a mustard plaster was slapped on your chest. The room was so hot you couldn't breathe and the plaster not only broke your congestion, it also removed the top six layers of skin on your heaving chest.

To loosen you up a little more, you were given a good dose of castor oil. What you didn't sweat out, you lost on your trips to the biffy until, in self-defense, you jumped out of bed yelling, "I never felt better in my life!"

Another winter cold preventative was unusual. Every home had a tin filled with water and creoline boiling all day and night on the old coal stove. This, it was said, killed all the germs in the air. I don't know if it actually worked its proverbial wonders or not but one thing it did was smell and so did all who breathed it in. By spring we could hardly handle fresh air!

I knew lots of mothers who hid their vitamin supply because kids craved them so much. One vitamin we took was Halibut Liver Oil. These were little gelatin capsules with the oil inside. We loved to crunch them and savor the oil. It makes me shudder to think of it now.

If we managed to find them, we'd really take on a feed. This overdose didn't cause any health problem, they just swept on through. What we did suffer from was a good hiding for using up the source of our well being. The Watkins man who sold them came only once every three months and mothers didn't want to run out before Spring.

The whole winter's supply for a family of six probably cost about the same as ten Fred Flintstone vitamins today. Yes, the cold might have been common back then but I'd say it's one of the most exotic of illnesses today.

Early Christmas Shopping

Each and every December, when I'm madly tearing about trying to find just the right gift for kith and kin, I vow, "Next year I'm going to do my shopping in October!"

Not only that, I'm going to have it all wrapped and ready in November and then I can spend December lolling about whistling Christmas carols! But of course, each and every year finds me up to my ears in wrapping paper, scotch tape and gifts the week before December 25th.

Now, that's not the absolute truth. There was one year I started shopping in January (if you can believe it). It didn't work out that well. The after-Christmas sales were on and I cut loose. With the five kids still at home I had the Family Allowance, which helped.

I actually made up a list and I really believed I had made some wonderful buys. I even took into consideration just how much each child would grow in 11 months. My, I felt smug!

I bought scented candles, bath oils, stationery, good books for some of the men and biscuits in fancy tins for those who had everything. These I hid in the deep freeze along with the chocolates.

Somehow, as the year progressed, the pile diminished. These gifts were handy for bridal showers and keeping Bill in aftershave and Ian and the girls in socks. Soon I found myself filching a dab of bath oil at the end of a hard day and using the pretty towels when we had overnight guests.

Of course, as I used the stuff I kept right on buying. I think it gave me a boost to tell the clerks I was finishing my Christmas shopping! I bought jeans for my girls, the really slim ones they loved. I attended bazaars and bought up aprons and doilies. I bought yarn by the pound to knit sweaters.

Either the tides were against me or my star sign was out because nothing worked out. In late November I piled what was left on the kitchen table. It was a dismal lot.

There were two boxes of stationery but half the envelopes were gone. The tin was all that remained of the English biscuits and what chocolates were left uneaten were pure white with freezer burn. The toffee had disappeared completely. (I found the empty tin stuck behind the toilet plunger.)

Those wonderful slim jeans I thought so perfect were out of style – something called "flares" had replaced them on the fashion scene. Even my Christmas cards had been taken to school for the card drive the Red Cross sponsored.

But, you know, in a way I was glad because the joy of the Christmas season for me is shopping for loved ones with the stores all decorated and Christmas music playing. I think it would be a dull, dull season if I couldn't shop.

I did have a couple of pretty organdie aprons left to send off to a friend. After Christmas, she wrote me a thank-you note and mentioned that she had actually made those aprons for the bazaar! I told her to give them to someone else and I'd send her some Hazelnut Swirls.

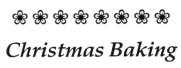

Christmas Baking

One integral part of the Christmas season for me is the baking. Each and every year I find myself stirring, whipping and turning the oven on right up until Christmas Eve or when my baking supplies run out.

I don't know why I get in such a tizzy over Christmas baking. Every single year I have a heart-to-heart talk with myself.

"No great baking bashes this year, just a few cookies and a pound cake and that's it!" If I find myself weakening, I carry on.

"Look, Bets (I always pay more attention if I call myself by name), we don't need all those calories. They are not healthy. Just crackers, vegetables, dip and cheese."

Still, every December finds me swooping around the kitchen, wooden spoon in hand and flour in my hair, acting madder than a mad scientist.

Actually, it starts in November when the store shelves are piled high with all those expensive ingredients in all their glory, exactly at eye level for the customer to drool over.

"Oh maybe two or three squares," I say to myself as I slip a few goodies furtively down into my cart. Before you know it, I'm knee-deep in ingredients and making triple batches of everything.

It's funny how Christmas baking has changed over the years. In pioneer times, women started early, in September, when the green tomatoes were brought in just ahead of a frost. It was then the green tomato mincemeat was prepared and put away in crocks in the cellar. This mincemeat is delicious and cheap even though it sounds weird to the cooks of today.

The all-important Christmas cake was baked about the same time. Not as elegant as the recipes of today, it was made of currants and raisins, a few cherries and peel, the latter being bought in chunks which the cook cut finely, not one piece bigger than a thumbnail. This preparation of the fruit took all day. Lots of butter and eggs went into the creation, along with things like grated carrot and possibly potatoes. A good shot of dark rum or whisky gave it additional flavor and helped keep the cake moist.

Carrot puddings, made of grated carrots and potatoes, were mixed in November. This sounds plain and rather dull but with spices, a few raisins and a hot brown sugar sauce poured overtop when served, carrot puddings matched any pudding you buy off the shelf today.

If you happened to have Scottish parents, a big "Black Bun" was also made. Those of other ethnic origins would all have their special Christmas baking treats.

But Christmas baking was to change. As time moved along, into the fifties and sixties, all the homemakers found themselves so busy there was no extra time to start thinking of baking in September for Christmas a good three months hence.

It was easier to buy exotic ingredients and people had the money to do so. This was the time of Nanaimo Bars and cookies you didn't have to bake. Christmas cakes were so classy you didn't know what you were eating and all you had to do was buy the ingredients and toss them in the bowl, no preparing peel, grating vegetables or whisking eggs by hand. In fact, this was about the time Christmas Cake mixes came on the market and many an old time cook had a slight stroke over these upstarts – much the same upset she had when Certo came along. One thing about it, all these goodies were rich and fairly rolling in calories. Carrot puddings? Heavens no! We could now buy the richest and best real plum puddings from England, no less!

But in the eighties we found ourselves more health-conscious and were into vegetables, dips, crackers and cheese and nuts. About the only sign of the good old pre-calorie days was a cherry pound cake, made with Country Crock margarine of course!

Many families held on to one or two traditional treats. Without that certain recipe, it wouldn't be Christmas. Our specialty was a cookie called "Snowdrops," a very old recipe I found in an obscure little magazine the first year Bill and I were married. I liked it. We were short of worldly goods, as they say, and this recipe called for only a modest amount of them. Rolled oats were the basic ingredient, with very few others. The whole thing was held together with water.

Now that first Christmas, Bill loved every ghastly thing I made and he made such a fuss over those cookies I felt I had to carry on each Christmas with a batch of Snowdrops.

I increased the batches to accommodate each new family addition until I was making not a triple batch but a sextuple batch! After a few years of this it became a distinct drag, however. They were tiddly things to make with all sorts of rolling in balls and dipping in sugar and I often found myself up into the night making enough to fill my preserving kettle. But I always hung a guilt trip on myself if I even thought about not making them.

"My family's needs are foremost. It just wouldn't be Christmas without Snowdrops." And I'd valiantly carry on. This went on for years. I was tempted the odd year to skip them but the Christmas spirit would always hit me below the belt and I made them once more. Actually, they tasted rather like wallpaper paste but everyone seemed to love them and they were a part of Christmas at Crocus Coulee.

Just three years ago, when most of my clan were sitting about at home having a visit, they divulged the truth.

"Mom, you might hate to hear this, but not one of us can stand Snowdrops. We used to flush them down the toilet. We never had the heart to tell you because you seemed to enjoy making them so much!"

So I made up my mind – wonderful – no more Snowdrops! I did wonder, though, what I'd do with all that spare time.

I've recently found another recipe which really sounds interesting and I THINK the kids will like it!

Hey Mom,
I'm the Virgin Mary!

Christmas Season is wonderful. Even in today's hustle and bustle there's still that special feeling, "spirit" if you like, that one gets only at Christmas.

I'm willing to bet no matter how exciting your Christmas, it doesn't begin to touch the joy felt years ago. Now I'm not speaking of 10 or 20 years ago – no, I'm talking about the old "horse and buggy" days, the days of homesteads and outdoor plumbing, back in the one-room school days.

Christmas was beyond words. No description could cover the joy, excitement and awe felt by kids and adults as well.

Possibly the most exciting time of all back then was the annual Christmas Concert. The anticipation started in November when the first thoughts and plans were being devised. Starting as a slight hum, by the day of the great event the air was so thick with excitement it would hit a 10 on the Richter scale.

The teacher would raid every bookshelf in the district, the local library if there was one and the city bookstore if she could get there. If all else failed, she wrote the skits herself. She always seemed to find just the right part for each child – quite a feat in itself. Imagine drawing eight grades of kids, of all sizes, sex and cultural background, into one program!

The atmosphere on the day the parts were given out was electric. Many of the girls clamored for the leading parts. Girls have always done this; it's the call of the stage! Even the shyest of them was so happy to be the prettiest little flower pot. The boys reacted differently. Even if they loved drama, it was corny to show it. So while the girls were squealing with delight, the boys were emitting great groans and rolling their eyes. Some teachers held auditions but each one knew full well which child she wanted in each role and often used the opportunity to bring her shy little introverts out of his or her respective shell.

Practising for the concert now became part of the curriculum. At first, for just a period or two a week; by December, it was by far and wide the most important subject and was practised every single day.

Besides the everyday rehearsals, there were other things to attend to. The backdrops had to be built and this usually fell on the shoulders of the older boys and the odd willing father. The girls took over the artwork needed on these creations. The curtains, usually a pair of old sheets dyed red or blue, were brought out and washed, then strung on a stout wire. Two little boys were assigned the duty of opening and closing them on cue – hopefully!

All costumes had to be homemade and some were a sight to behold. They were made of some amazing things, yet on that night they were perfect. Old curtains, chicken feathers, bits and pieces from everyone's closet. What they lacked in authenticity, they made up for in imagination.

While teacher and pupils were preparing for the event, mothers busily sewed the all-important Christmas dresses. The boys were quite content to have a bath and wear their Sunday pants and shirt but each girl just had to have a new dress.

If the year was good the parents might have been able to buy special material from Eaton's catalogue. If it had been a lean year, the mother would improvise. Often an old dress of her own was brought out of the old trunk, taken apart, pressed and sewn into a lovely new creation.

The candy bags, one for each and every child, were filled with a few old-fashioned hard Christmas candies, an orange and a few nuts. Each little brown bag was tied securely and set aside.

The tree was decorated and the last dress rehearsal run through. These often bombed. Nerves were frayed and lines forgotten, however the teacher always stated, "A poor rehearsal always means a triumphant concert. Don't worry, you will do me proud!" The children believed her because they wanted to.

That night every little girl went to bed with her newly-washed hair tied in a hundred rags so each ringlet would be perfect and the older girls heated their curling iron in the cookstove. When the iron was red hot, they applied it to their locks quite gingerly, hoping they would curl and not smoke!

As each family arrived at the school, they gasped in delight. The school had turned into a fairyland, the Christmas tree shone and the air filled with magic.

Each play and recitation went perfectly. Angels sang the songs and even the curtain pullers, who got in a fuss and fell off the stage, received resounding applause.

As the last carol was sung, Santa arrived in all his mystery to pass out the gifts and candy bags. The gifts were simple, a hairband, a book, a ball. Even so, each one was received with squeals of delight.

Too soon it was over and the little school was left dark and quiet. But all the children slept with bittersweet memories and wonder that night.

'Tis the Day After Christmas

'Tis the day after Christmas and down on the farm
All creatures are resting, both bovine and human.
The wrappers are scattered all over the floor,
There's tinsel and ribbon stuck to the door.
The dad looks content in his easy chair,
Reading about Reform and how it will fare.
The mother, God bless her, is resting her feet -
The very first chance she's had in a week.

The children are playing, not with their toys
But instead with boxes and wrappers with joy.
The house is a shambles but nobody cares.
There's marks on the floor and there's spuds on the chairs.
The larder is full with some wonderful stuff,
Leftovers aplenty – I'm sure there's enough.
The turkey looks bedraggled, all stripped of his meat,
But what's left on his bones will still be a treat.

Some friends and neighbors drop in for a spell
To have a good visit and wish us all well.
The silage's been fed and the stock bedded down,
Let's go view the bright lights aglow in our town.
Then the family will gather and chat about things,
There's peace and contentment which holidays bring.
Christmas Day is exciting and blessed 'tis true,
But the day after Christmas has its blessings, too!

❀ ❀ ❀ ❀ ❀ ❀

My Fur Coat

❀ ❀ ❀ ❀ ❀ ❀

I'm a rather contented person with only a few real wishes. The one big want in my life, which I've harbored for years, is to own a fur coat. Many of my friends are absolutely aghast but I can just feel it draped over my shoulders, light, soft and warm.

Now the style of my dream fur changes with the times but the longing for one remains. At first I thought I'd like a stole or a short cape. Back then I showed off my legs and thought I'd be absolutely devastating in a pencil-thin short skirt under the fur.

Later on, my dream was a fur jacket. This was during my thrifty, "get lots of wear out of it" years. Then if the skirt lengths dropped or rose I could still wear my fur. I would wear it with a silk shirt and I'd lift the collar at the back and wear my hair up in a dramatic upsweep.

But of course, with five kids and a farm to keep going, the sensible part of me prevailed and I bought sturdy, serviceable, cloth coats, in styles I could be comfortable in. I remember one I bought in Zeller's for $20.00. I actually tried it on, bought it and carried it out in less than 20 minutes. I wasn't too excited over it but it was a lovely blue and big enough to wear whether in a pregnant state or not (this state took up a great deal of my life in those early years).

Later, when the skirt lengths plunged, I cut the coat off to car coat length, dyed it black and tossed a plaid scarf over the shoulder. I was set for another four years. When it started to look a little shabby, I just smiled to myself and said, "Never mind, wait 'til I get a fur."

Oh, I've had fake furs over the years and they looked great. In fact my trousseau coat was a fake leopard which I thought quite elegant. I've also worn a fake Persian lamb jacket which I liked. Deep down in the core of my being, I knew I wanted a real fur.

I haven't a clue where this wish sprang from. Maybe the old movies when all the movie queens would be photographed climbing out of cars all fluffy in furs or maybe it was some magazine or other which caught my eye. I know I never craved jewels and I couldn't care less about gowns but a nice fur sends shivers up my spine.

Oh, I fully understand it's downright dangerous to own a fur coat in this age of animal rightists. You and your coat are in great danger out on the street. It's a jungle out there. These people wouldn't even look up if you murdered a whole school class but when it comes to an animal, watch out. But this doesn't phase me.

If I ever have a windfall or my lucky star shines, I'll be off to buy my fur. I'll wear it too, come hell or high water and heaven help any misguided rightist who approaches me and my coat.

Mmm, maybe a nice coach length. I'll wear an elegant black outfit under it and I might even don mascara for the occasion.

I just hope it happens soon. I'd hate to die and have it draped over my coffin like the flag is for veterans!

Winter Weight Removal

Every single March finds me in the same predicament – 10 pounds heavier than last fall. To add insult to injury, the new fashions are in every magazine and store window in all their glory, while visions of me trying them on with my extra rolls are in my nightmares.

So I drag out what is called a Gut Buster from where I retired it under the bed and proceed to try to undo all the wrongs I committed over the long winter months.

I bought this thing at a flea market. The girl on the box looked so svelte I knew I wanted to look like her. I couldn't afford a rowing machine and I've seen so many exercise bikes being used for coat racks I figured this thing was more my speed. The first few days I huff and puff my way through 10 sit-ups. In a couple of weeks I've worked up to 50 or so. This beats wearing what used to be called a girdle. I can handle a soft shaper but I've had some bad experiences with girdles.

I remember when my kids were all little and I needed a girdle like I needed a case of lockjaw, I still wanted to be slimmer. So I went and ordered a girdle from the catalogue. Packed in a box about the size of a match carton, it looked much like the thing our grandmothers hung on the wall and stored string in for household jobs.

I hid the girdle under the bed until after supper when I knew the rest of the family would be watching TV. I was taking no chances on one of the kids using the experience for Show and Tell the next day. I slipped into the bedroom – the very last bit of "slipping" I did that night, I might add. I tore the box up in fifty thousand pieces and buried it in my underwear drawer and then proceeded to turn myself into a model.

With the first immense tug I got it over my ankles. I tugged and tugged and finally got it to my knees. Had I been sent the wrong size? I crawled out of it and had a look at the label. Nope, it was right, so I had to start all over again.

Part of the trouble was it stretched out in some spots and not in others, so when I grabbed a good handful the rest stayed back and bedded down. As I got bits and pieces up I began to resemble a partly-inflated balloon. I scattered dusting powder here and there on my sweating skin so it would slip up easier but no luck. By now my hands kept slipping and hitting me in the jaw.

I finally got it up and over one shoulder only to discover, to my horror I had it on inside out! So I had to repeat the whole performance again, puffing, wiggling and groaning. I hadn't realized I was making weird noises until Bill tapped on the door to see if I was ill. I didn't have enough breath left to answer him.

The next day I took the ghastly thing and pegged it out on the closet wall not unlike the way you peg a coyote hide on a barn. This helped stretch it a bit so I could wear it once or twice. When I did my voice always rose three octaves!

I never bought another one. Instead, I'm still using the Gut Buster gizmo and with perseverance hope to hold my own. I also watch the gate while Bill feeds silage, walking about swinging my arms to put in the time. I know I resemble a galloping goose trying to take off in a wind but it's for a good cause!